OSPREY COMBAT AIRCRAFT • 68

F-117
STEALTH FIGHTER
UNITS OF OPERATION
DESERT STORM

SERIES EDITOR: TONY HOLMES

OSPREY COMBAT AIRCRAFT • 68

F-117 STEALTH FIGHTER UNITS OF OPERATION *DESERT STORM*

WARREN THOMPSON

OSPREY
PUBLISHING

First published in Great Britain in 2007 by Osprey Publishing
Midland House, West Way, Botley, Oxford, OX2 0PH
443 Park Avenue South, New York, NY, 10016, USA
E-mail; info@ospreypublishing.com

ISBN: 978 1 84603 182 3

Edited by Tony Holmes and Bruce Hales-Dutton
Page design by Tony Truscott
Aircraft Profiles and Scale Drawings by Mark Styling
Index by Alan Thatcher
Originated by PDQ Digital Media Solutions
Printed in China through Bookbuilders

07 08 09 10 11   10 9 8 7 6 5 4 3 2 1

For a catalogue of all books published by Osprey please contact:
NORTH AMERICA
Osprey Direct, C/o Random House Distribution Center,
400 Hahn Road, Westminster, MD 21157
E-mail:info@ospreydirect.com

ALL OTHER REGIONS
Osprey Direct UK, PO Box 140 Wellingborough, Northants, NN8 2FA, UK
E-mail: info@ospreydirect.co.uk
www.ospreypublishing.com

CONTENTS

INTRODUCTION

Aviation technology advanced rapidly during the 1950s. So rapidly, in fact, that by the time a new type had become operational it was ready for an upgrade, if not almost obsolete. Then, in the 1960s, the USSR perfected the surface-to-air missile. It quickly became the key defensive weapon, forcing strategic bombers originally designed to operate at high altitudes down to treetop level if they were to stand a chance of flying a successful bombing mission. From this change of tactics terrain following radar (TFR) evolved, and with it the F-111. This complicated system suffered its share of problems when the jet was rushed into action over Vietnam in 1968. Although three aircraft were lost in rapid succession, the technology prevailed. TFR, together with variable-sweep wings leading to higher speed, soon became accepted by both sides in the Cold War.

The conflict in Vietnam had shown to the West that the European members of the communist bloc were not the only countries able to effectively deploy batteries of SAMs supported by radar-controlled automatic weapons. Indeed, by 1972 Hanoi's defences were considered to be on a par with those of Moscow. During the conflict the United States Air Force (USAF) had lost 2256 aircraft, of which 1737 were directly attributable to combat. Only a small percentage of these losses resulted from encounters with hostile fighters. The heaviest losses were suffered by F-4 Phantom II and F-105 Thunderchief units, which were assigned some of the most dangerous targets.

It was during the mid 1970s, with the bitter experiences of the Vietnam War still very much in the minds of senior US military officers and politicians alike, that thoughts turned to ways of designing an aircraft whose surface could absorb probing radar beams or deflect them in such a way that there would be little or no return. This would expose even the most heavily defended targets to air attack, especially at night. Thus, the concept of Stealth technology was born, and the end results were to be dramatic. Compared with the dangerous missions flown by F-4 and F-105 crews over North Vietnam, the achievements of a handful of F-117s over Baghdad during the first few nights of Operation *Desert Storm* in January 1991 seem almost unbelievable.

Despite its long and debilitating war with Iran, Iraq was considered in 1990 to have the world's fourth largest army. Assets included 7000 radar-guided missiles, 9000 infrared missiles, 7000 anti-aircraft guns and 800 fighter aircraft. Some ballistic missiles were also thought to be capable of carrying chemical and biological warheads. This was not a threat to be taken lightly. It was also known that the Soviet Union had spent nearly $235 billion on perfecting an integrated air defence system for the Iraqis, who had sufficient funds available to acquire such advanced technology. As a result, Baghdad had probably become the world's best-defended city by 1990.

Against such a background, it is hardly surprising that Coalition forces spent so much time building up their strength before *Desert Storm*. Virtually every weapon in the American arsenal, with the exception of the B-1B bomber, was to be utilised. And included in the force poised to eject Iraqi troops from Kuwait was the F-117.

A study of the available literature on Lockheed-Martin's Nighthawk, especially that describing the type's combat activities, soon reveals that few photographs were taken and little video footage shot during stealth operations in *Desert Storm*. Any histories published now or in the future will, therefore, have to rely on the personal recollections of those few pilots who flew in combat to illustrate the aircraft's role in the campaign. They relied on stealth, flawless execution of the mission plan and absolute precision bombing to get the job done.

The text in this volume includes personal interviews with the pilots who conducted these missions, which were always flown at night in a subsonic aircraft that was invisible to the enemy's defences. A common thread running through these recollections is their praise of the Mission Planning Cell (MPC). The effective management of this in-theatre asset was critical to the jet's success, and survival, in one of the most dangerous environments ever encountered. The MPC's importance can never be overstated, hence its frequent mention in this book.

The F-117 pilots were not involved in exciting dogfights, nor did they shoot down any enemy aircraft. Nevertheless, by the end of *Desert Storm* they had logged close to 7000 hours of combat time and delivered more than 2000 tons of bombs – all without receiving so much as a scratch. This is their story.

Warren Thompson, Germantown, Tennessee, December 2006

TOP SECRET

*H*ave Blue – two seemingly innocuous-sounding words that combined to provide the codename assigned to a programme which involved a level of secrecy not seen since the early work on the atomic bomb in World War 2. The F-117 Nighthawk's elaborate design and futuristic features also required some of the most extensive engineering and test work ever done on an aircraft.

The origins of the stealth concept can be traced back many years, with British scientists being the first to note that radar had limitations in detecting wooden gliders. Northrop's ill-fated Flying Wing – forerunner of the B-2 Spirit stealth bomber – also proved difficult to detect during flight at Edwards Air Force Base, California, in the late 1940s.

Experiences during the Vietnam and Yom Kippur wars, when Soviet-designed radar-directed air defence systems took a heavy toll of attacking aircraft, prompted US military planners to seek ways of reducing, if not eliminating, the radar signature of aircraft. The Russians themselves also played a key role in the development of stealth technology, but without being aware of it. A paper published in an obscure Soviet journal described a method of calculating radar cross-sections of aircraft. This article caught the eye of a Lockheed engineer, and the method's feasibility was duly tested by the company's famous Skunk Works. The rest, as they say, is history.

The *Have Blue* programme, which involved the design, construction and testing of two aircraft intended to test stealth technology, was initiated in 1976. The first made its maiden flight on 1 December 1977, but was subsequently destroyed in a crash on 4 May 1978. Despite this setback, *Have Blue* led directly to full-scale production of the F-117A (in a project codenamed *Senior Trend*), the first prototype of which completed its initial flight on 18 June 1981. Production began in

This F-117 is undergoing final assembly at Lockheed's Skunk Works in Burbank, California, during the late 1980s. Engine systems, the jet's sharp-sloping nose, flight control surfaces and avionics were all added at this stage in its construction process *(Lockheed Martin)*

October 1983, and averaged eight aircraft a year. The production run ended when Lockheed had built 59 jets, with the final airframe being delivered to the USAF in June 1990 – only two months before Iraq invaded Kuwait.

The 37th Tactical Fighter Wing (TFW) would be the only USAF organisation to operate the F-117 in *Desert Storm*. The unit was officially activated on 5 October 1989, although training operations from the top secret base at Tonopah, in Nevada, were already in progress by then. The unit could trace its lineage to the secretive 4450th Tactical Group (TG), which had been formed in October 1979 in preparation for the F-117's service entry in August 1982. Four squadrons would eventually fly the aircraft from Tonopah as part of the 4450th, prior to the unit being inactivated when the 37th TFW was established.

Just two months after the 37th was activated, its aircraft were involved in the December 1989 Panama crisis, codenamed Operation *Just Cause*. Although the F-117's participation was brief, it left no doubt about the aircraft's ability to deliver ordnance with pinpoint accuracy. The Panamanians lacked a sophisticated radar network, however, so this deployment was not considered to be a true test of the aircraft's stealth capabilities.

During the early years of F-117 training at Tonopah, all flights by stealth fighters were made under the cover of darkness. This not only maintained secrecy, but also prepared the pilots for future combat missions, all of which would be flown at night. Here, two F-117s taxi out for an early evening training mission soon after the jet's existence was declassified *(Denny Lombard/Lockheed Martin)*

EARLY OPERATIONS

The training operation at Tonopah was intense, but restricted to a relatively small geographical area, especially in the early days. Most of the wing's aircraft were in the air every night, and as the experience level of pilots and planners increased, the F-117s began to operate beyond the practice ranges, but always during the hours of darkness.

The training at Tonopah was rigorous because most missions required precision hits against a variety of targets on the range at night *(Lockheed Martin)*

Several talented individuals were involved in mission planning and execution during this secretive phase of the F-117 programme. Of all the names mentioned during conversations with pilots on these topics, the one that cropped up most frequently was that of Maj Dale 'Sledge' Hanner. When each pilot checked out on the F-117 he was assigned a 'bandit number', signifying admission to a highly select group. Hanner's was 239. He joined the programme in 1987, and was appointed chief of weapons and tactics before his final year with the

unit. Hanner also participated in Operation *Just Cause*. His recollections provide an insight into the Nighthawk's 'black' operations out of Tonopah at the time the F-117's capabilities were being honed;

'To get to our highly classified base, you would have to cross 150 miles of desert, pass through two guarded entry control points and a double fenced area that could only be accessed via a palm reader. Once this far, you had to negotiate the cipher lock on the squadron door

Because of its high landing speed, the F-117 has to utilise the braking power provided by a drag 'chute, as seen here (*USAF*)

and walk into a safe, which in turn sat inside another larger walk-in safe.

'Aircraft hangar doors were never opened until 30 minutes after sunset. Taxiing out could be a little tricky because you were not allowed to use the taxi light, as this could accidentally illuminate another F-117. Often, this meant pulling into the arming area and then rolling out to the runway in total darkness, except for the blue taxiway edge lighting. If a truck had happened to get in your way you would not have seen it until you collided with it – and it is doubtful that the driver would have seen you either. Happily, this never occurred. It was a real relief to get airborne in these zero light conditions.

'There was a strict rule that all aircraft had to be down at Tonopah by 0330 hrs so that everyone could be in place with all the doors nailed shut by first light. This rule was brought in following investigations into some earlier accidents within the 4450th, which were related to the fact that the pilots were exhausted from the gruelling routine of five nights of hard flying, and then catching up on their family life for 48 hours at the weekends. The routine of getting your head down before the sun came up meant that pilots got more restful sleep. It was even better in the summer, when the days were longer and flying time shorter.

'We were given high priority when we flew, especially if we had some kind of inflight problem that meant we couldn't get back to Tonopah. This would mean diverting to a major air base and getting the kind of treatment reserved for the SR-71 during its formative years in the 1960s.

'We carried an official letter when we flew which was addressed to the most senior officer present – usually the wing commander – saying that if we had to land at his base (we were mostly captains at that stage), and even if heavily outranked, the colonel or whoever was to consider us his boss for whatever we might need. The letter was signed by the USAF chief of staff. Keep in mind that the existence of the F-117, and what we were doing with the aircraft at Tonopah, was still only known by a privileged few. I believe that all the wing commanders at bases close to where we operated, such as Hill, Mountain Home and Beale AFBs, were given an advance heads-up on what to do if we had to land.'

MISSION PLANNING

The most important aspect of all Nighthawk training, and future combat, was the mission planning. From modest beginnings when the jet entered

Col A J 'Tony' Tolin commanded Tonopah stealth operations until the eve of Operation *Desert Shield*. He was succeeded as CO of the 37th TFW by Col Alton Whitley on 16 August 1990. This F-117 was assigned to Col Tolin during his time as wing CO, and it is seen here parked in a hangar at the top secret Nevada base
(Eric Schulzinger/ Lockheed Martin)

Capt Mike Riehl works out the details of a mission in the simulator. Riehl, (Bandit No 320) saw action during *Desert Storm* after becoming fully qualified on the F-117 on 1 November 1989 at Tonopah
(Denny Lombard/Lockheed Martin)

frontline service with the 4450th in 1982, planning had been honed to a science that would reach maturity in early 1991 when stealth aircraft faced the much-vaunted integrated air defence system that defended Iraqi airspace.

Standard F-117 mission planning typically saw each squadron provide a pilot to the MPC on a nightly basis. Once aloft, these same individuals would lead other aircraft from their unit in missions where jets usually flew an identical route for six to ten minutes (six minutes in the summer, when the nights were shorter) at a time in trail. Hanner, who was heavily involved in the MPC during his time on the F-117, recalled;

'The aircraft were at last cleared to fly off-range just prior to my tour commencing, and the route devised by the group would typically consist of a 600-mile loop around California or Utah. We also did some loops around the Nellis range complex. The mission lead would pick seven or eight targets, and photos of them would be produced for each pilot. A typical target might consist of a tool shed behind the ninth house down from the fifth block down from an intersection in central Sacramento, California! A "hit" required certain criteria to be met that would ensure that a real bomb, assuming it guided correctly, would strike the aim point.

'Because the squadron hit rate was consistently so high – Capt David Russell (Bandit No 215), for example, went a year-and-a-half without missing a target – and because the competition was so extreme, the mission lead usually picked the most difficult targets. I picked targets that I subsequently missed, knocking me out of the wing's "top gun" competition for that quarter.'

Although F-117 tactics evolved in the same way as those for any new aircraft, mission planners had to take into account two factors that were unique to the Nighthawk – all operations would be flown at night, and the aircraft's key defensive weapons were its invisibility to radar and the naked eye.

Throughout the 1980s, every pilot took a turn at being mission lead at least once a fortnight. Such rotation provided crews with an opportunity to learn how the full potential of this new weapons system could be realised. Although the 37th TFW's MPC sessions involved pilots working up highly complex mission scenarios, the participants in these flights were blissfully unaware at the time that less than

18 months after the wing was created, they would be sent to strike targets protected by some of the most formidable air defences ever devised.

There were many constraints placed on the pilots participating in these flights, including minimum altitudes for safe terrain clearance during peacetime, single-aircraft only training formations and a limitation in the types of weapons that the F-117 could then carry. Maj Hanner explained how pilots worked within these restrictions in order to get the job done;

'Some mission leads took what they were given, picked targets and planned a route similar to what had already been done. Others tried to brainstorm better ways of defeating the defences and killing the target. Then they tried to come up with plans for doing so while still complying with the rules. My job as chief of weapons and tactics was to stimulate thinking and discussion and to encourage innovation. But ultimately it was up to the mission lead to do the grunt work of conceiving and planning the mission.

'We also came up with innovative tanker operations during this time, expanding on communications-out procedures, which we were able to use in Operation *Just Cause,* and covert tanker fly-by/pick-up procedures. I don't think that we ever actually used the latter because such a mission profile used up a hell of lot of the tanker's fuel.'

It was during this formative period that the complicated planning involved in going from single aircraft to multiple F-117 attacks was perfected. The real benefit in multi-plying the number of jets simultaneously sent out to attack targets would not be realised until the first few nights over Baghdad.

The 4450th TG focused its attention on going after small targets during its night practice missions for much of the 1980s, although most sorties during this period often saw the same ranges being worked over in Nevada. These early flights were also unrealistically short in comparison with the missions that would be flown by the F-117s in wartime. Such restrictions were amongst the reasons why the

When the sun set at Tonopah, the time for serious business began. This F-117 has been loaded either for a clandestine mission over the range or for a sortie involving a simulated bombing attack on a target hundreds of miles from its home base. Either way, it had to be back before sunrise *(Denny Lombard/Lockheed Martin)*

Long before they flew the real thing, F-117 pilots had extensive sessions in the flight simulator at Tonopah. Here they could experience situations that they were likely to face in combat *(Denny Lombard/Lockheed Martin)*

Although the secret was already out by the end of 1988, all F-117s remained at Tonopah (where this photograph was taken) until mid 1992. The stealth fighter was officially revealed to the public at Nellis AFB in April 1990 *(Denny Lombard/Lockheed Martin)*

Before the F-117's public debut, security was extremely tight both at Lockheed's Skunk Works and at Tonopah. During the day, steps were taken to ensure no Soviet satellite or telephoto lens compromised the weapon's secrecy *(Lockheed Martin Skunk Works)*

Department of Defense finally relaxed the security surrounding the jet on 10 November 1988.

With the USAF having 'gone public' with the Nighthawk, the 4450th TG could at last access a considerably larger training area in which to conduct its missions. This in turn meant a wider variety of 'targets' to prosecute, although aim points still had to be reached and returned from by first light.

Capt Mark Renelt (Bandit No 264) flew on a number of the early extended-range missions, including one which took the F-117s east of the Mississippi River;

'Our first flight past the river was a round trip to the Eglin AFB ranges over in the panhandle part of Florida which lasted more than eight hours. If I remember correctly, we had six Nighthawks and two tankers working the mission. Planning was interesting because most agencies weren't used to dealing with us. The people at Eglin didn't have a lot of target pictures, so we made runs based on what was available over their range. We began the mission with a tanker pick-up, and this was designed to ensure minimum exposure to prying eyes and radar.'

The tankers overflew Tonopah as the Nighthawks took off so that they could be joined up before leaving the base's traffic control area. As a result, controllers would see just the two tankers flying in close proximity. After join-up, the group would climb out of the restricted area. The Eglin mission was uneventful, with the tankers bringing the F-117s in from the Gulf of Mexico, due south of their targets. They then set themselves up for a multi-ship attack on a simulated airfield. Once that was completed, the Nighthawks departed to the east, before turning south to the Gulf and a rendezvous with the tankers. From that point, the F-117 pilots faced the long flight back to Tonopah, landing before sunrise.

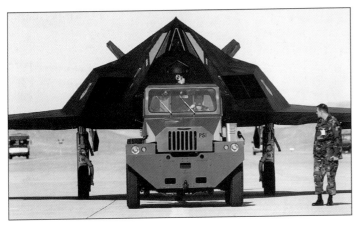

The F-117's maximum speed is about 600 mph (970 kmh) but its service ceiling has never been revealed, and its optimum bombing altitude also remains classified. The aircraft's wing span is 22 ft 6 ins (6.8 m) (*Denny Lombard/Lockheed Martin*)

One of the pilots involved in these long-range missions was Maj Wesley Wyrick (Bandit No 330), who subsequently flew many combat sorties over Iraq in 1991. He was also one of the first pilots to deploy to Saudi Arabia with the 415th TFS as part of Operation *Desert Shield* on 26 August 1990. Wyrick recalled some of the specifics of these training sorties for the author;

'The training routes had a wide variation, but in general they proved much tougher to hit than actual wartime targets during *Desert Storm*. The mission planners would target houses, shopping centre complexes and government buildings, plus the standard stuff on the ranges like aircraft hulks in revetments. However, the MPC's all-time favourite target was the plastic "Tuff Shed". These were small utility sheds sold in Nevada, and they usually measured 1.5 x 3 metres in size. Most were placed in backyards under a tree. These sheds were low infrared gradient targets which didn't show up well since there was very little temperature difference between them and their surroundings. We also regularly targeted the 4450th TG commander's house at Nellis.

'The target sets ranged from government and industrial buildings in Sacramento down to electrical junctions and petroleum stores. On one "turkey shoot" night that I can vividly remember, the MPC chose a telephone booth as the target just to make things interesting.

Aircraft 86-0837 of the 37th TFW was specially posed for a Lockheed Martin photo-shoot at Tonopah just months prior to its deployment to the Middle East. The name of Capt Matt Byrd (Bandit No 348) is displayed below the canopy. Christened *HABU II*, this aircraft would subsequently log 37 combat missions over Iraq (*Denny Lombard/Lockheed Martin*)

'In an effort to keep us on our toes, some of the targets in the towns were also "late shows". This meant that they were difficult to line up because they didn't come into the pilot's view until just seconds before the bomb was due to be "dropped". These were the toughest missions to fly, with targets only appearing when you were almost on top of them. You then had just seconds to line your aim point up and make the drop. The target could be on the opposite side of a mountain that you were flying over, or in a valley below a ridge line. Target acquisition and tracking time was significantly compressed as a result.'

But as Maj Wyrick added, it was targets like these which gave the F-117 pilots the sharp edge they were later to demonstrate during *Desert Storm*.

DESERT SHIELD BUILD-UP

Despite the ongoing tensions between the Arab world and Israel, the Middle East was calm in July 1990. As there were few, if any, indications of what was about to happen, 2 August 1990 can be compared to 25 June 1950. Then, all had seemed normal on the Korean peninsula immediately prior to the North Korean Peoples' Army crossing the 38th Parallel to begin an offensive against its southern neighbour. Forty years later, Iraq's unprovoked invasion of Kuwait generated the same kind of outrage throughout the world.

In August 1990, after Iraqi dictator President Saddam Hussein had unleashed his massive military on an unsuspecting Kuwait, US President George H W Bush was quick to put his country's forces on alert for a rapid response. He wanted a quick and decisive military commitment, but he was also determined to avoid the mistakes of the Vietnam War. This meant minimal political interference to enable the commanders in the field to call the shots. As a result, Gen Colin Powell, Chairman of the Joint Chiefs of Staff, Gen Norman Schwarzkopf, head of US Central Command, and Lt Gen Charles A Horner, commander of the latter organisation's air forces, would have the final word on strategy.

During the spring of 1990, discussions at the Pentagon had concluded that Iraq's eight-year war with Iran (which had ended less than two years earlier) would require a lengthy period of reconstruction of its armed forces before they posed a serious threat in the region once again. Nevertheless, the Central Intelligence Agency (CIA) kept the country under close surveillance, and by the third week of July its operatives were reporting that Iraq had positioned 30,000 troops along the border with Kuwait. By month-end estimates of troop numbers had swelled to 100,000. When questioned about this build up, the Iraqi ambassador claimed that it was either a normal movement of forces or military manoeuvres. The CIA, however, stated that an invasion of Kuwait was imminent. The agency had no idea how soon that would happen.

At about 0100 hrs Middle East time on 2 August, Iraqi forces made a quick and brutal thrust into Kuwait. US reaction was immediate

Preparation for the initial deployment to the Middle East for Operation *Desert Shield* was a massive undertaking. When the aircraft departed Tonopah, they were loaded with bombs in case Iraq attempted a sudden invasion of Saudi Arabia. Replenishment by KC-10 and KC-135 tankers was necessary not only for the flight to the Middle East, but also for all combat missions once in-theatre *(Eric Schulzinger/Lockheed Martin)*

because the Bush administration feared that Saddam Hussein would order his troops into Saudi Arabia in furtherance of his ambition to control all the region's oil reserves.

Appropriately, the first US fighter unit to deploy to Saudi Arabia was the 1st TFW, which arrived at the Royal Saudi Air Force Base (RSAFB) at Dhahran on 7 August 1990 following a non-stop flight from its home at Langley AFB, Virginia. It was just one of numerous units that the USAF mobilised in the first ten days following the invasion, Military Airlift Command being kept busy moving troops, and their equipment, into forward areas. Figures released after the war by the Pentagon showed that USAF sorties flown in the Middle East went from zero in early August to more than 150 per day by mid-month, peaking at about 200 during September and October as troops and equipment poured in.

On 13 August, less than a week after the 1st TFW had arrived in Saudi Arabia, the 37th TFW received classified Travel Order TJ-013, instructing it to send one of its three squadrons, and 22 jets, from Tonopah to the Middle East. Being the Atlantic component of the stealth fighter community, which meant that it was expected to 'chop' to US European Command (and, as in this case, CENTCOM too) in time of war, the 415th TFS was duly chosen as the first F-117 unit to deploy to Saudi Arabia for Operation *Desert Shield*. This unit had also provided six F-117s and pilots for the 19 December 1989 *Just Cause* strike on Panama.

The 415th commenced sending its jets to King Khalid RSAFB, near the city of Khamis Mushait, on 26 August 1990, with orders to respond to any Iraqi aggression once in-theatre as directed by CENTCOM.

The departure of jets from Nevada was the culmination of 13 days of frantic planning by squadron commander Lt Col Ralph W Getchell and his operations officer, Lt Col Barry E Horne (Bandit No 314), along with their supporting staff. Both men had begun preparations for the move as soon as they had received their orders on the 13th, and they quickly encountered a problem that would plague scores of other units over coming months – insufficient tanker support. It was impossible for the tanker force to meet the level of demand placed upon it within so short a timeframe, and for the 415th this meant a 48-hour delay in its departure. The USAF had already committed 32 tankers to the Middle East, and at its peak on the eve of *Desert Storm*, this force would exceed 300.

One of the 415th TFS's Nighthawks lands at Langley AFB after completing the first leg of the unit's deployment to Saudi Arabia on 19 August 1990. The 415th was the first stealth fighter squadron to respond to the *Desert Shield* call to arms
(Denny Lombard/Lockheed Martin)

NEW WING CO

On 16 August 1990, Col Alton Whitley assumed command of the 37th TFW from ex-4450th TG CO, Col Anthony Tolin. As Bandit No 150, Whitley topped the list of experienced F-117 pilots within the wing. Receiving the 37th's deployment orders hours after assuming command, Whitley found himself aboard an eastbound C-5 Galaxy nine days later. He shared the jet with one of the wing's most valuable assets – the mission planning

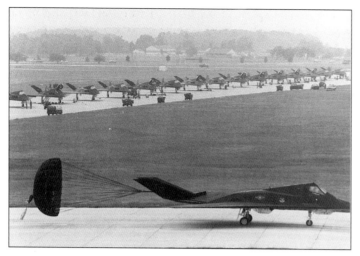

The 415th TFS flew 22 Nighthawks from Tonopah to Saudi Arabia via Langley AFB, and the stopover in Virginia provided the news media with its first opportunity to take pictures of so many F-117s together in a single group. The aircraft were parked overnight on an inactive runway while their pilots rested in preparation for the long final leg of their flight to the Middle East (*Julie Lidie*)

system. Recalling that hurried departure, Col Whitley said;

'Ralph Getchell was also on board the C-5, and he did an excellent job of bringing me up to speed on his unit's capabilities. It was during that deployment that he suggested the title of "Team Stealth", which we would use throughout our time in *Desert Shield* and *Desert Storm*. We headed straight for Rhein-Main AB, in Germany, and from there made a non-stop flight to King Khalid RSAFB. We arrived only minutes before a C-141, which was carrying additional personnel, equipment and supplies for the 37th TFW. From this point on we started getting everything up and running in preparation for the first squadron of F-117s to arrive.'

Maj George I Kelman (Bandit No 281) was one of the pilots chosen to fly a jet to Saudi Arabia, and he told the author;

'From Tonopah, we headed for Langley AFB. We parked our F-117s on a dead runway, which allowed for some very impressive pictures to be taken of our squadron en route to the Middle East. That evening, we went into some detailed briefing sessions and prepared to take-off again the following afternoon. The weather at the time of our departure was very bad, with rain and low cloud ceilings.

'Our support tankers were coming out of McGuire AFB, and I was leading the last six-ship of Nighthawks from the 415th.

'We got airborne and the military controllers weren't much help when we were trying to join up with our tankers over the water. I had to cycle back and forth between the tanker and my wingman so I wouldn't lose him. Our six-ship was taking evasive action by going around clouds and still trying to stay as close to the track as possible. We finally broke out of the bad weather about ten minutes before we would have had to turn around and return to Langley. Those 40 minutes were the most demanding part of that entire ocean crossing to Saudi Arabia. We spent more energy in that time than we did for the rest of the flight.'

The squadron encountered no further trouble during its long journey to the Middle East, with the aircraft meeting up with another group of tankers over Gibraltar. Several pilots remarked that once in clear weather, their toughest job was changing the batteries on their Sony Walkman! The view from that altitude was spectacular as they turned over Egypt and the Red Sea, but as they approached their destination they faced a new problem. The pilots had no information about radio frequencies for their new base, and the Saudis knew very little about the F-117s' arrival. Finally, the 415th's support personnel had flown in less than two hours ahead of the main force, so there had been no time to prepare the base for the jets.

Yet despite the recent arrival of the groundcrews, Maj Kelman still found King Khalid RSAFB buzzing once he had taxied in after landing;

'When I touched down, I found that things were really hopping on the ground! As soon as we landed, we were told to taxi into our hardened aircraft shelters (HASs). Our groundcrews were ordered to get our jets ready to fly combat missions within 24 hours. For all we knew, we would be bombing Iraq that night! But this did not happen. We were really beat by the time we arrived at our base. Some of us had to be helped out of the cockpit by the enlisted guys that were around the aircraft. I remember that after I climbed down, somebody handed me a "near beer". We had been in the cockpit for 17 hours, and in the air for 15 of those, and all we got for our efforts was one "near beer". I guess it could have been worse.'

Maj Wesley Wyrick was another pilot involved in the crossing;

'When we left Tonopah, we were already loaded with maximum ordnance because we didn't know if we would be flying combat within a few hours of arriving. We came into the Middle East ready to fight. We had no idea that we wouldn't get the opportunity to use our bombs for several months. In the meantime, there were several problems to solve as we settled into our new base at King Khalid. We did little or no flying during our first six weeks in Saudi Arabia. As a squadron, our biggest problems revolved around when we would go into combat and trying to make sure we had enough spare parts to keep our aircraft in the air.'

Once in Saudi Arabia, and with the imminent threat of invasion having diminished, the squadron's MPC set about creating a training syllabus that would keep pilots at the peak of their proficiency as they waited for *Desert Shield* to be replaced by *Desert Storm*. Maj Kelman was heavily involved in this aspect of the deployment;

'We immediately set up a training scenario as we decided on our tactics, and how best to work ourselves into those tactics. We were going to do things a little differently than the way we had done them back at home, as we planned on carrying out mass attacks once the war started. In order to prepare ourselves for such missions, we had to practise getting a number of jets over one target area in as short a time as possible. When we first started flying these sorties, we would take 15 to 20 seconds to get all of our bombs off against one target area. However, by the time our practice missions were in full swing, we had reduced that figure to just six seconds.

'This effectively meant that we could put as many as 12 aircraft over a single target area, and all their bombs would impact within six seconds. It took about six weeks of intense repetition to accomplish this spacing, as all of our training was being done under the cover of complete darkness.'

As the training tempo increased, the Saudi Arabians agreed to open up a disused bombing range for the F-117 squadron to use. Much effort was expended by the 415th to make the site usable, and Maj Kelman was given the job of range officer. He related to the author one of the

Making a test hop after routine maintenance, this 37th TFW(P) F-117 is seen over a Saudi resort area north of King Khalid RSAFB in late 1990. It took the stealth pilots about two-and-a-half hours flying time just to reach the Iraqi border from their base – part of the reason why their combat missions during *Desert Storm* were so long in duration *(Rob Donaldson)*

more unusual challenges facing him in his new post;

'We were having trouble keeping the native Bedouins off the range, especially at night. Things got so bad that I had to helicopter out onto the range to have a meeting with the tribal chief. Since we did all of our practice at night, we had a dangerous situation developing. I tried to explain to him that we were bombing on the range at night, and that his people would not be able to hear us coming. I suggested that they not use the range road, and that it would be safer to take the long way round.

Flanked by two of his groundcrewmen, Capt Wes Cockman (Bandit No 318) poses at Langley AFB on 2 December 1990 during the 416th TFS's overnight stop en route to Saudi Arabia. By the time Cockman had completed his tour on the F-117 some months after *Desert Storm*, he had flown 450 hours in the Nighthawk (Rob Donaldson)

Lined up in squadron strength, these 416th TFS Nighthawks were photographed by Capt Cockman at Langley AFB en route to the Middle East to join their sister squadron at King Khalid RSAFB. They would be in place and ready to fly missions on the first night of the *Desert Storm* air offensive (Wesley Cockman)

'No matter how I tried to explain it, it just did not sink in. There were many nights when the guys would have to pull their bombs off the crosshairs to avoid hitting a Bedouin. Most of the time they were in vehicles crossing the range. Fortunately, we didn't have any accidents involving the tribesmen and our bombs.'

Whilst the unit was training, the MPC continued to work up the target set for the first night of *Desert Storm*. Much of this planning relied on intelligence being fed to the 415th by other Coalition assets, and the quality of this information was often variable, as Maj Kelman explained;

'In the preparation for the war, during the *Desert Shield* period, there were a lot of personality conflicts up at the higher levels of command which initially meant that we did not receive the best information that we could have. So, we were forced to get hold of the intelligence that we required in a roundabout way. We sent messages home via satellite to retrieve the necessary data which allowed the MPC to be effective.

'The F-117 team was dedicated in its mission to acquire the very latest intelligence, as without the latter, the stealthiness of the aircraft, and the

route planning that allows the jet to make the most of this unique feature, is greatly compromised. The fact that we survived all of the missions flown in *Desert Storm* without suffering a single casualty was a testament to that ability to acquire the intelligence required.'

BACK AT HOME

With the 415th deployed, the remaining pilots from the 416th TFS and the 417th Tactical Fighter Training Squadron (TFTS) waited impatiently for their call to arms. The 416th TFS was the Pacific component of the 37th TFW, being earmarked for operations with US Pacific Command in the event of war. However, it had sent a handful of pilots and jets to Saudi Arabia in support of the 415th's efforts, leaving the remaining elements of the unit to fly simulated combat missions based on feedback from its sister unit. One of the pilots kicking his heels in Nevada was Capt Mike Mahan (Bandit No 323);

'Preparations for the upcoming war from the viewpoint of the 416th TFS grew rapidly once the 415th started feeding back information. We had little to go on until October, however, but once the information started to flow, we got all the intelligence we required. We used it to shape the training missions that we were flying out of Tonopah, doing our best to conduct mirror sorties matching those being flown in Saudi Arabia.

'We worked hard to improve on the skills and tactics that we would need if we deployed. As it turned out, the tactics that we had been perfecting at Tonopah prior to Kuwait being invaded were exactly what we needed to fight in *Desert Storm*. This meant that we did not have to alter the way we were flying the jet in order to accomplish the mission.

'Despite quickly realising the similarities between our peacetime training missions and the combat sorties that we would eventually fly, my squadron still pumped the 415th for all the information it could provide us with prior to our deployment. And once we all realised that we would be conducting missions over enemy territory that were identical to our training flights, we really began to "put on our war faces" for our final sorties from Tonopah. Yet despite taking our training missions very seriously, nothing could prepare us for the sheer amount of bullets and missiles that we would have to face over Baghdad.'

The initial cadre of 415th TFS pilots to deploy to King Khalid RSAFB pose in front of one their jets soon after arriving in Saudi Arabia in August 1990 *(Rob Donaldson)*

On 2 December the 416th FS commenced its deployment to Saudi Arabia following the receipt of movement orders. Recently-appointed CO Lt Col Greg T Gonyea was in the vanguard of the transatlantic crossing, his unit taking advantage of the lessons learned during the 415th FS's deployment almost four months earlier.

In August, pilots had flown from Tonopah to Saudi Arabia, via Langley, which was a gruelling ordeal for them. To avoid a repeat of this, experienced instructors from the 417th TFTS flew the 416th FS aircraft to Langley on the 2nd, where they were met by frontline pilots brought in from Tonopah by transport aircraft. Fully rested ahead of the long over-water flight, the crews from the 416th departed Virginia on the 3rd. Despite encountering bad weather en route to the Middle East, the unit successfully made it to Saudi Arabia without any problems.

Capt Mike Mahan (Bandit No 323) participated in the crossing;

'Being the 416th FS's mobility officer, I had to attend to all the packing and preparations for the move. Our flight was fourteen-and-a-half hours long. To this day, that was the longest flight I have ever recorded, and I have no desire to duplicate it – especially in a single-seat fighter! There were 13 aerial refuellings for each jet during the course of the flight. We used KC-10 tankers, and there were two F-117s assigned to each one. Most of the refuellings were done in total darkness, as we had trained for at Tonopah. The sun came up as we were over the Azores, and it made for an impressive sight from our altitude.'

Maj Rodney L Shrader (Bandit No 312) was also a participant in the transatlantic crossing;

'I was in the same flight of F-117s as our wing commander, Col Al Whitley, on the way over. Once we launched out of Langley and cleared the poor weather, our flight was pretty uneventful. After about eight hours of the tight quarters inside the cockpit, I was ready to start banging my helmet on the side of the canopy, wanting to get up and stretch.

'The most spectacular event was when the tankers handed us off, at night, in the middle of the Atlantic Ocean. Being stealth pilots, we never chattered much on the radio, but we could listen to those guys manoeuvring into position. It took about 30 minutes to switch out, and then we were back on the boom again.'

HIT THE GROUND RUNNING

Once in Saudi Arabia, the 416th TFS had to quickly bed down so as to be prepared for combat, which, unbeknownst to the pilots, was now only a matter of weeks away. Shortly after the squadron arrived in-theatre, the 37th Tactical Fighter Wing (Provisional) was activated to oversee all F-117 operations from King Khalid RSAFB.

Reflecting on the early stages of the deployment, squadron CO Lt Col Greg Gonyea recalled;

'While we had been preparing for the move, the 415th FS was making a Herculean effort to get its pilots ready for combat. On top of that, the food they were eating was lousy and the quarters cramped. Some of this was attributable to the fact that King Khalid was a brand new air base with a lot of kinks still to be worked out.

'When the unit arrived in early December, we had no idea that the war was still several weeks away. The squadrons were competing against each other for space, living quarters, recreational space and so on. Two full combat squadrons require a lot of space. It was a real turf war. We were the new kids on the block because the 415th had been there for four months. When the war finally started, it was only fair that the 415th should fly the first sorties, because those strikes on Baghdad would definitely be the "glory" missions for the USAF and the 37th TFW(P).

'Each squadron had been fully briefed on what its targets were going to be during the first three days of the war. Our Intel folks knew what had to be taken out early on, and their list of targets went through very few changes. That was the way we practised. Once we received this information, I took up our guys in pairs. They were assigned specific targets, and it was handled on a team basis. I spread out the experience level so that more seasoned pilots were working with newer aircrew.

'My objective was to make sure that there was no difference between the crew rosters for the first and second nights. This ensured that if somebody fell sick or something happened to prevent that pilot flying, his partner would be capable of stepping in and completing the assignment. It had to be a buddy system, and there was no A or B team.'

One of the 416th TFS's most experienced pilots was Maj Rodney Shrader, who started working in the MPC upon his arrival in-theatre.

'The MPC was run by the weapons officers from each squadron. We rotated several of the guys in and out of there, and I was privileged to work with some of the most professional people in our wing.

'For much of *Desert Shield*, staff in the MPC spent their time reviewing the first strike missions. Upon receiving our target assignments, there was a flurry of activity as we studied the routes and available photographs. It was important to have the attack plans buttoned up as soon as possible. The mission profiles had mostly been set up by the 415th TFS, which had been in-theatre far longer than us. Our pilots would come into planning every day to make sure they had the most up-to-date photos and target data. At this time, there was no way to tell exactly when the war would start, so we had to keep up with any changes in the game plans.'

The group MPC was to be the eyes and ears of both squadrons. It was located in a small mobile container next to the Intel van in a large concrete hangar. This meant that any data and pictures from satellites were immediately made available to them. But it was clear that the biggest threat the pilots would have to face when they penetrated Iraqi airspace and headed for their targets would be the SAMs and AAA.

There would, however, be a general misunderstanding about these stealth missions, which arose from the terminology used. Much of the news media coverage implied that the F-117s were deployed in 'waves'. This is partly true, but some clarification is needed. The aircraft usually took off in pairs, meeting the tanker together en route to Iraq. Once they topped up their tanks, the pilots were on their own to carry out their assignment. Most pilots held the rank of captain or major, so were experienced enough to take full advantage of the jet's advanced systems. And it would take a lot of maturity and discipline to fly those missions.

TESTING THE ENEMY

Aside from conducting training flights over the ranges in the weeks leading up to *Desert Storm*, the 37th TFW(P) also probed Iraqi defences by conducting sorties close to Iraq. Capt Rob Donaldson (Bandit No 321) of the 415th TFS recalled the details of these flights;

'All of our training flights were flown within the borders of Saudi Arabia, although on several occasions we flew all the way up to the Iraqi border – 2.5 hours flying time from King Khalid. These missions were flown in an effort to test their reactions to our presence in the area. It was the flights up to the border

that were a real morale booster for all of us. There were no indications that they were ever aware of our being in the area! However, when other non-stealth aircraft types came into the same vicinity, they immediately heated up the Iraqi radar scopes – the enemy knew these jets were heading their way some considerable time before they reached the border.

'In the wake of these flights, we all began to realise that when the war started we would be able to ease right into our assigned targets completely undetected. Our degree of confidence was very high as a result.

'Another important facet of those final long-range training sorties was executing numerous hook-ups with our tankers. We followed exactly the same routine that we would use in *Desert Storm*. Fly up to the border, top off, and then instead of heading east, we would fly back to King Khalid. The Iraqis became very comfortable with this.

'There was one thing we had going against us during this period, and also in the first few weeks of the war – unpredictable weather. It would cause us a lot of trouble when it came to identifying our targets. The weather also made it difficult for us to stay close to our tankers in zero/zero visibility. Also, hanging onto the boom at barely 300 knots proved to be challenging to say the least. We eventually overcame this particular problem by having our tankers increase their speed. After months of training, to say that we were all ready to take it to Iraq would have been an understatement!'

Lt Col Gonyea also flew several of these practice strike sorties;

'The types of missions we flew along the Iraqi and Kuwaiti borders were conducted in order to lull the enemy into a false sense of security. Firstly, we had to find out if they could see us. If they could, then we had to find out what they were capable of doing. By repeating these sorties over and over, if they could see us, then the Iraqis figured they knew exactly what we were going to do. Then, one of these days, we were going to do something totally different and they were going to be caught off guard – that is what happened on the night of 16 January 1991.'

A KC-135 tanker refuels one of the Nighthawks somewhere over northern Saudi Arabia at dusk during a training sortie in December 1990. When its tanks were replenished, the F-117 would probe the Iraqi border area, before turning south for the long flight back to King Khalid RSAFB (Denny Lombard/Lockheed Martin)

King Khalid RSAFB was the newest air base in Saudi Arabia at the time of Desert Shield, having been built to house some of the most modern military aircraft in the Saudi inventory. It had been deliberately sited as far as possible from Iraq and its Scud missiles. HASs, like the one seen here, were built to withstand considerable punishment. Note both US and Saudi flags hanging from the HAS roof (Rose Reynolds)

FIRST NIGHTS OVER BAGHDAD

As the 37th TFW(P) prepared for the launch of the air offensive that would signal the start of Operation *Desert Storm*, its pilots knew they faced a powerful enemy. Intelligence estimates made on 17 January 1991 had put the strength of the Iraqi Air Force (IrAF) at 750 combat aircraft, with an additional 200 supporting types. Of this total, the MiG-23 was probably the most numerous.

Intelligence sources also stated that Saddam Hussein's air force operated from roughly 24 main air bases and 30 dispersal fields. The bunkers and HASs housing many of the IrAF's combat aircraft had been

built by German, French, British and Yugoslavian experts, and they were designed to withstand anything short of a nuclear explosion. All of these bases were defended by a formidable array of anti-aircraft artillery (AAA), which would have constituted a death trap for any American fighter-bomber attacking during the day.

The Iraqis were also estimated to have at least 16,000 radar-guided and heat-seeking SAMs ranging from Vietnam War-era SA-2s to more modern SA-16s. And then there were the defending fighters. Dealing with the latter would be the responsibility of the USAF's F-15C Eagles units in-theatre. The pilots assigned to these air superiority squadrons

Locked, loaded and ready, this F-117 has been parked outside its hardened shelter at King Khalid. Its two LGBs will be retracted into the bomb-bay once inspected by the pilot prior to engine start *(Ken Huff)*

Weapons specialists go through the final stages of arming two Nighthawks that were involved in the first wave of attacks on Iraq on 17 January 1991 *(Wes Cockman)*

were keen to take on their Iraqi counterparts, although they were unsure about the level of resistance they would encounter.

Responding to up to date intelligence reports detailing the sheer size of the integrated air defence network in place in Iraq, the 37th TFW commenced a series of exercises on 3 October 1990. These were designed to hone pilot skills and build confidence within the aircrew that they could indeed prosecute targets successfully, despite the enemy defences. *Sneaky Sultan* was the name given to this operation, which also enabled wing CO Col Whitley and his staff to exercise

plans and procedures for devising missions, interpreting intelligence data, preparing mission folders, loading weapons and simulating the launch and recovery of 'waves' of F-117s.

Exercises such as this were vital to the Nighthawk pilots, as aside from Col Whitley, only Col Klaus Klause (director of operations) and ex-A-10 pilot Maj Rod Shrader had previous combat experience. Even so, Vietnam veteran Whitley had great confidence in the personnel under his command, as he explained;

'While few of our pilots had been tested in combat, we were blessed with some of the most talented aviators in the Air Force. I knew that they were well trained, and supported by some of the most capable people available. We also knew that very few people understood our weapons system, and its unique capabilities, as well as its limitations. To put this into perspective, I believe the first time that Gen Horner and some of the other high ranking officers in US Central Command Air Forces (CENTAF) ever saw an F-117 was during their initial visits to our deployed location.'

As the 37th TFW(P)'s CO, Whitley disclosed what was uppermost in his mind during the days leading up to the first night of combat;

'I had frequent flashbacks to scenes in old movies about World War 2, where the senior officer comes into a large briefing room to give the crews their assigned targets for the day. Our briefings were of a similar nature. Most of the assignments throughout the war were against critical targets in heavily defended areas.

'The setting for the first two waves on the opening night of the

Security at King Khalid was very tight, for although the base was located out of Scud missile range, there was still the possibility of a terrorist attack *(Wes Cockman)*

Lt Gen Charles A Horner (far right), commander of all Coalition aircraft in *Desert Storm*, is briefed by 37th FW(P) CO Col Alton Whitley (far left) at King Khalid *(Rose Reynolds)*

war included a room full of exceptional young professionals who were razor sharp and ready, willing and able to meet their tasking. However, on that first night the big question was, of course, "what if stealth technology doesn't work?" Personally, I had no reason to believe it wouldn't. But I also knew the technology wouldn't make us invisible – just hard to detect and certainly difficult to track. Testing is a necessary step in the development of any system, but you never know how effective a combat system will be until it is tested under actual frontline conditions.'

After almost five months of preparation and wondering when the action was going to start, it still came as a mild shock when the orders arrived on 16 January 1991. Maj Jerry Leatherman (Bandit No 259) was heavily involved within the MPC. He and many other F-117 pilots had found it difficult to adjust to the long working hours since their arrival at King Khalid. Leatherman would be up all night in the planning cell, after which he would finally go to bed somewhere between 0500 and 0600 hrs. Of course once the war began the MPC

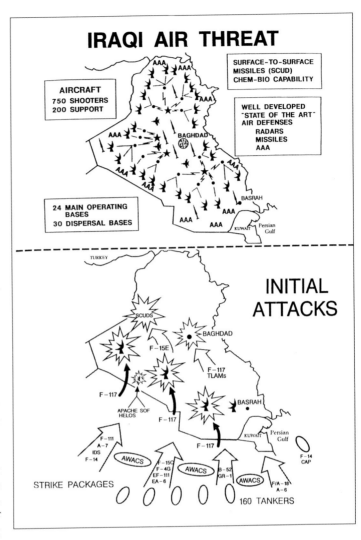

These CENTAF diagrams from 1991 reveal the threats facing Coalition aircraft on the eve of *Desert Storm* (top), and how the Iraqi defences were engaged in the first 24 hours of the war. Note how the F-117 attacks cleared the way for conventional strike aircraft to penetrate the heart of Iraq

would be manned 24 hours a day until the last mission of *Desert Storm* had been completed.

Maj Leatherman was just getting off to sleep after yet another long night in the MPC working the mission assignments for Night One of the war when he was roused at 1000 hrs and told that Col Whitley wanted to see him right away;

'I got half dressed and went over to the colonel's office. He handed me a piece of paper that read, "Execute Wolf Pack – H-Hour is Zero One Zero Zero Zero Zulu". This translated to 0300 hrs Baghdad time. He and Col Klause asked me if we were ready. I said I was, and that I'd better go and wake Maj Joe Bouley (Bandit No 331) and his team because they were the planners for the first night. Since I was participating in that first attack wave, I couldn't both plan a mission and fly it – you did one or the other.

'The first night of the war went pretty much as planned, with Joe Bouley and his guys putting the final touches to the missions such as exact times for the flow to coordinate with the tankers and updates from the Intel people on the exact placement of threats such as AAA and SAMs. Having woken him up and got the rest of his people to work in the MPC,

I then went back to try and get the rest of my much-needed sleep because I knew that at 0100 hrs the following day I was going to be somewhere over Iraq. If I needed anything right now, it was rest.

'By the time I got up a few hours later, the first kink in the plans had surfaced, and it pertained to the tanker support. The times that they had set up for us didn't match what we were requesting. I finally had to make a call to the tanker wing and tell them that they belonged to us, which meant that they had to be where we needed them at the time we'd requested. We transmitted the times to them and they were right there where they were supposed to be when we were ready to refuel.'

The first-rate facilities at King Khalid were virtually brand new when the F-117s arrived. In fact parts of the base were still in the final stages of completion in late 1990. Its HASs could easily accommodate two F-117s, meaning that all maintenance and service work could be done in a totally safe environment *(Denny Lombard/ Lockheed Martin)*

TO WAR

The first wave of ten jets to depart King Khalid launched at 0026 hrs, and watching their departure was Maj Wesley Wyrick. As the 415th TFS's assistant operations officer, he performed the function of 'ramp rat' for this first mission, being ready to assist both air- and groundcrews should there have been a problem with any of the primary jets;

'It was extremely interesting to watch something as complicated as this come off like clockwork. For all of us on the ground, it was a tense period. Once all of the guys got airborne we had no more contact with them, so we had to depend on CNN to find how we did. We knew exactly where every aircraft was headed, and the second they were to be over their targets. It was amazing how well it went. We had a group of very disciplined pilots. Everything we did was based on precise timing. The pilots came out to their aircraft, got in, started the engines and waited for their time to move out into position.

'From that point on it was like watching a ballet at night. Aircraft were taxiing out at certain times, coming from all over the base, and from

This Nighthawk has been towed out of its two-aircraft shelter at King Khalid so as to allow its groundcrew to finish off their pre-flight preparations *(Wes Cockman)*

opposite sides of the runway. Each pilot knew when he was to move out, and there was no radio transmission between the tower and our F-117s. They would line up side-by-side at the end of the runway and, at a set time, throttle up and take-off. Another pair would then pull up into position.

'There were no radio transmissions made throughout this period, the departures being made "comm out". It would be radio out for ground operations, radio out for departure and then go up and hit the tanker, again radio out. The first transmissions from the jets would be made when they were heading

south after the strike, usually as they crossed the Iraqi/Saudi border.'

The first F-117 strike wave flew its mission under the pressure of countless unknown factors, combined with complete radio silence. The pilots 'stealthed up' by retracting their antennae immediately after take-off, and they were still radio silent several hours later when they cleared hostile territory. Although trained for perfect execution, the aircrew involved were still taking a new aircraft into one of the most dangerous environments in the history of war. The top command in-theatre had predicted losses, but just how many was another unknown factor.

Col Whitley had been granted permission to fly that first night by his boss, Lt Gen Horner, but on condition that he would initially be on the ground to ensure the first wave was launched safely. Once this was done, he could fly in the second wave. Whitley repeated that there would be no way of determining results or losses until just before each pilot returned to base, when they were permitted to break radio silence to report.

FIRST STRIKE

There is some controversy about which weapons were the first to hit Iraqi targets, thus signalling the start of *Desert Storm*. A handful of Tomahawk Land-Attack Missiles were launched from ships within range in the northern Arabian Gulf, before the first wave of F-117s arrived at their targets. Maj Joseph R Bouley, who was a key participant in the MPC, has no doubt about the actual sequence of events. He recalled;

'I stuck around during the opening night of the war after the first wave had launched at 0026 hrs. When all the aircraft were off and en route, a large crowd gathered in the pilot's lounge to watch CNN. We watched the results with the entire world as it happened. It was an emotional feeling to see all the lights in Baghdad go out. It was very clear to all of us that the planning and execution had worked perfectly.

'To set the record straight, the Tomahawk missiles didn't make the first hits on the Iraqi capital. Official records I've read state that the first wave of Tomahawks struck Baghdad at 0305 hrs. Two of our F-117s hit radar sites just 50 miles inside Iraqi territory at 0251 hrs. At 0300 hrs sharp,

On the war's opening night, Iraqi command and control centres, together with key radar sites, were targeted twice to ensure that outlying airfields had no way of knowing what was happening over Baghdad. Within 48 hours most of these targets had been destroyed and the enemy's individual military units were effectively on their own *(Eric Schulzinger/Lockheed Martin)*

Col Alton Whitley took over as 37th FW CO on 17 August 1990, leaving him no time to settle in before the unit's initial deployment to the Middle East for Operation *Desert Shield*. At the time of his appointment, he was Director of Fighter Training and Tactics at another base. He led F-117 operations throughout *Desert Storm (Lockheed Martin)*

eight jets hit targets in the city centre. At 0400 hrs, the second wave of Nighthawks hit, with ten jets in the strike package, followed by the third wave, in which I participated. My target was one of the major radar sites. Within a couple of hours Iraq's military had been all but blinded.'

The 0251 hrs strike referred to by Maj Bouley saw Maj Greg Feest (Bandit No 261) and Capt David Francis (Bandit No 317) knock out a critically important Interceptor Operations Centre, the destruction of which helped open up a radar-free corridor that conventional jets could safely pass through on their way north. The centre, housed in a protective, hardened bunker, was the key link between radar units sited along Iraq's border with Saudi Arabia and the main air defence headquarters in Baghdad. Capt Francis recalled his participation in this historic mission;

'We were taken out to our jets from the crew area by shuttle bus, and as each pilot was dropped off at his shelter, he shook hands with all the others. In the back of our minds, we all wondered who would return and who would not. After all, we had been told to expect two or three F-117s to go down on the first night.

'My jet was 86-0821, which carried the name *SNEAK ATTACK* on the inner face of the nose gear door. I knew that it had been specially chosen for this mission due to its very good stealth signature, but that that could be quickly taken away by one missing piece of RAM (radar absorbent material). With this fact firmly in mind, I thoroughly inspected the outside of the F-117 with a flashlight. This inspection revealed no problems, so I climbed in and started the engines. Everything checked out fine. Now all I had to do was wait 35 minutes before I could taxi out.

'Finally, we took off. Everything went just like we had trained. We found the tanker on time, got our gas and started heading north. Shortly after the first refuelling, my FLIR (Forward Looking InfraRed optical sensor) went blank! This wasn't good, as the FLIR was used for finding the target well ahead of the pilot reaching the delivery point. From the altitudes we were using on this mission, the target did not appear in the DLIR (Downward Looking InfraRed optical sensor) until less than one minute prior to us "pickling" (releasing) our bombs. For big, easy to identify targets, there would have been no problem, but for my first one – an earth-covered bunker – it would be cutting it very close.

'I tried everything to get the FLIR working again – turning it off, letting it cool, and then turning it back on again. I did this at least five times, with absolutely no success. I finally decided to go with what I had.

Maj Joe Bouley suits up for another mission. When he was deployed to Saudi Arabia with the 415th TFS during the very early days of *Desert Shield*, he was one of the less experienced F-117 pilots, with only about 50 hours of Nighthawk time. Nevertheless, Bouley flew on the first night of the war, when his targets were a fortified command bunker and a nuclear facility in south-east Baghdad *(Joe Bouley)*

A 37th TFW(P) Nighthawk emerges from its parking area en route to the main runway at King Khalid for a late night or early morning mission. This action photograph was taken before the second or third attack wave, because the first would have left while it was still light *(Denny Lombard/Lockheed Martin)*

If something had to break, I would rather it be my FLIR than my DLIR. If the latter had gone out I would have turned around and headed back to base because there would have been no way to point my laser at the target, which meant that the laser-guided bombs carried by my jet would have gone "stupid".

'We took our final top-off of fuel and dropped away from the tanker. Feest left first, and I watched as his dim lights went out and he disappeared into the darkness. My concentration was fixed on running through the seven-step check to ensure that the jet was in its most

F-117 pilot Capt Wes Cockman (centre, in flying suit) is pictured in discussion with squadron maintenance personnel soon after returning from a mission to Iraq. Cockman took a number of the photographs featured in this book *(Rose Reynolds)*

stealthy configuration. I must have double checked my light switch a dozen times! It was poorly designed – a three-position switch, with "off" in the middle. If you accidentally clicked it down instead of to the centre, your lights were on dim. It was almost impossible to see from the cockpit, and very hard to bend your head down under the canopy rail and see the switch position, so I flicked it up and down several times to ensure that I was feeling it in the middle position.

'We had a pretty short run to our target of not more than 15 minutes. I was very careful to stay right on my timing because I didn't want to get too close to my lead. I couldn't do much searching for the target with my FLIR, so I looked out of the cockpit a lot. It was pitch black in front of the aircraft. At precisely 0251 hrs, Feest's bomb hit, which put him nine minutes ahead of the first strikes against Baghdad. I saw his bomb explode in the upper portion of my DLIR screen, which gave me an excellent pointer to my target, since I knew where my bunker was in relation to his.

'Suddenly I noticed a lot of white flashes in the air in front of me. His bomb blast had alerted the Iraqi gunners that an attack was underway, and the AAA was coming up. It seemed like it was heavy, but it was my first experience at getting shot at. In the days to come, I would find out what heavy AAA was really like!

'I studied my screen intently, and as I finally located my bunker in that sea of sand, I pressed the pickle button. I could feel the bomb-bay doors open and the sudden jolt as the bomb came out. Then I just concentrated on holding the cross-hairs right on the target. About four seconds before impact, it became apparent that I was tracking the left side of the bunker instead of the top. An adjustment was made immediately and the bomb hit right on the roof. It looked just like all the

A KC-135 boom operator's view of an F-117 as it is refuelled near the Saudi-Iraq border in late January 1991. This operation was undertaken in complete radio silence during *Desert Storm* *(Rose Reynolds)*

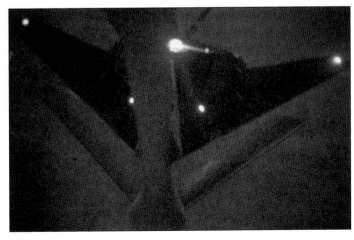

Even though King Khalid RSAFB at Khamis Mushait was out of Scud missile range, precautions against chemical warfare attack had to be taken. Here, 37th TFW(P) conduct decontamination drills *(Rose Reynolds)*

In the 43 days during which F-117s flew combat missions in *Desert Storm*, they established a record that would be hard to surpass. They represented the ultimate 'force multiplier' because of their success in destroying targets which would have seen losses to Iraqi defences if attacked by jets such as the F-15 and F-16, which have a distinct radar profile. This shot was taken from a KC-10 prior to the F-117 heading into Iraq at dusk *(Rose Reynolds)*

bombs I had dropped during countless practice missions – a black star erupted in the centre of my scope, but I was able to see smoke coming out of the doors of the bunker. Obviously, it was a perfect hit.

'It was a relief to know that I had done my job, and that the F-15Es behind me could now get through to their targets. I turned west and headed for my second target.'

BAGHDAD

Pilots who flew with the 415th and 416th FSs on one of the three waves during the first night of combat in *Desert Storm* can recall virtually every detail of their flights in the early hours of the morning on 17 January 1991, yet some of the later missions seem to blend into a combination of several others. Col Whitley is one of those individuals to have a clear recollection of that first night, as he told the author;

'The most memorable aspect was the density of the city's defences. It was like nothing I'd ever seen before. All the other things involved in flying the mission such as take-off, tanker rendezvous, ingress and targeting were all normal, and no different to what we'd practised. But the explosions at and above my ingress altitude, as well as the intensity and density of the AAA below me, will always be remembered!

'Baghdad appeared as a dull orange glow on the horizon when I was pretty far out. Yet as I got closer, the glow became an intense fireworks display. The closer I got, the more I doubted our ability to fly through it and survive. When I was directly over the city, the bright flashes of the rounds exploding illuminated my cockpit. I could feel the concussions and hear the explosions. Eventually, the skies became so saturated with enemy fire that the flow of 100 per cent oxygen in the cockpit couldn't overcome the aroma of gunpowder. Frankly, I held little hope that all our aircraft and pilots could come through this unscathed. Believe me, it was an eye-opening experience.'

During the first nights of the campaign, stealth pilots reported seeing enemy aircraft airborne near their assigned targets. However, none of the MiG and Mirage F1 pilots realised just how close the F-117s were. Maj Bouley, who was in the third wave on 17 January which was launched late that afternoon, was one of those to spot IrAF jets over Baghdad;

'I showed up at operations at 1430 hrs. By 1600 hrs we were ready to go out to our aircraft and launch the third wave for the opening day of the air war. This would be an unusual sortie, it required two of us to fly in close proximity. I would be flying with 415th TFS operations officer Lt Col Barry Horne. Basically, we were going after the same target, but we would hit it about one minute apart, and I would be following Horne.

'I thought that there would be a lot of excitement in preparing for these missions, but it was rather quiet. Our guys were ready, and we had had plenty of time to prepare. We went over to Life Support to get our gear. Those guys were worried about us, and they had everything ready and double-checked to make sure it was in perfect working order. When we arrived on the flightline, our groundcrews were all over our aeroplanes. The munitions personnel were making sure everything was good to go with our bomb loads. One last glance at my target photos and I was ready. We launched at 1739 hrs, which left us plenty of daylight as we made our way across Saudi Arabia en route to Iraq.

'We were in for a six-hour flight because our targets were in the extreme northwest corner of Baghdad. It was a well-fortified bunker command post that would require the big GBU-27 deep penetration weapons to destroy it. That would take one of my bombs. The second weapon – a GBU-10 – was destined for the big nuclear facility in Baghdad, which was the same one that the Israelis bombed back in the early 1980s. They put it out of business, but it had long since been rebuilt, and there was an enormous berm built around it.'

After a 45-minute flight from King Khalid, the two F-117 pilots met their first tankers. They would top up their fuel again at the border, which was still over an hour away. Crossing into enemy airspace, they 'stealthed up' by retracting all antennae. Timing was critical, and they were right on schedule, with Horne a minute ahead of Bouley. However, they then hit trouble when the expected 35-knot headwinds suddenly turned into a 100-knot gale. This forced both pilots to fly faster, which in turn caused them to be a little late at the turn points. Fuel consumption was greater than expected too. And despite being invisible to Iraqi radar, the pilots worried that enemy fighters might be up that night. Maj Bouley continued;

'I don't know whether Lt Col Horne ever saw them or not, but about 60 miles inside Iraq, I spotted two MiG-23s with my FLIR. They were heading west in formation, and probably flying a combat air patrol between the Saudi border and Baghdad. They never saw either of us.

The F-117 has a distinctive silhouette from any angle, and its multiple facets are easily recognisable in this overhead view. The aircraft represented a considerable achievement by Lockheed's engineers and designers but it took skilled pilots to fly it in action and to execute the battle plans to perfection *(Denny Lombard/Lockheed Martin)*

An F-117 returns to King Khalid shortly after dawn to signal the end of yet another long combat mission over Iraq. The jet's night vision telephoto capabilities (FLIR/DLIR), combined with its ability to project a laser beam onto the target to ensure clinical ordnance guidance, made the aircraft one of the most accurate weapons for precision bombing in the US arsenal *(Rose Reynolds)*

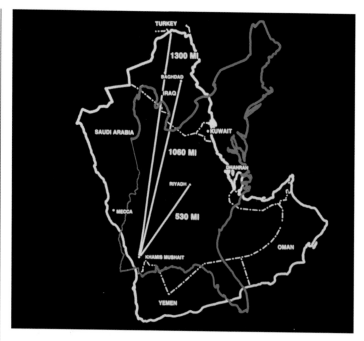

This map shows how far the F-117 pilots had to fly to reach their targets – note the overlay of the eastern USA, from the east coast as far west as the Mississippi River, which gives some idea of the distances being covered by the 37th TFW(P) on each and every mission. On their return to Saudi Arabia, some pilots left hostile territory extremely low on fuel. This meant that F-117s had to be topped up virtually over the Iraqi border, and this required careful coordination with the tankers to ensure that they were in position ahead of the Nighthawks' arrival
(Rob Donaldson)

'We continued west and then moved over to the extreme north-west corner of Baghdad, before turning in the direction of the target. I made a right-hand descending turn to reach my prescribed bombing altitude. The city was no problem to locate. It could be seen from a great distance because it was lit up from one end to the other – the action had already started. AAA was everywhere, with an occasional SAM fired straight up. Using my FLIR, I could see several aircraft flying around, but they were too far away to tell if they were ours or theirs.'

There is little doubt that the weather was the Iraqis' greatest ally during *Desert Storm*. Although on this occasion there was concern that it might not be suitable over Baghdad, conditions turned out to be good enough around the targets for accurate drops to be made. Of greater concern to the pilots was the volume of AAA being fired at random into the night sky – Maj Bouley had to lower his seat to avoid being distracted by it. Although surrounded by ribbon tracer, Bouley guided his first bomb into the centre of the bunker that he was targeting, and then set course for the southeast corner of the city. He subsequently reported;

'I was about 12 minutes away from my second target, and concentrating so hard on finding my initial points for my run in, looking at the target photos and getting the weapon ready, I simply disregarded the shooting. There were tracers everywhere! I picked the nuclear facility up on my FLIR when I was about two minutes away. The nuclear reactors were so big and so hot that they showed up clearly on my scope. There was never any doubt about the target. I saw Horne's bomb explode on the target. Seconds later, I was in a perfect position and "pickled" off my GBU-10. I guided the bomb down for a direct hit and then got out of the area as soon as I could. When we arrived back at base, a crowd was waiting. Although we flew the aeroplanes, it was a team effort.'

TARGETING THE INVISIBLE F-117

By the end of the first day of *Desert Storm*. it was evident that Iraqi radar could not detect the F-117s. Nevertheless, the sites that had survived the initial onslaught that marked the start of the aerial campaign were doing their level best to aid in the shooting down of a Nighthawk. Radar operators could detect USAF tankers orbiting over the Saudi border, and assumed that they were refuelling the F-117s, as no other returns were received. When the tankers turned away, the Iraqis concluded that the 'invisible' bombers had crossed into their airspace. Timing the gap between that event and the first bombs falling on Baghdad would, they reasoned, be when they should start firing in the hope of hitting something. Capt James R Mastny (Bandit No 268) explained;

'During the first couple of days of the war, when we were sending wave after wave of Nighthawks over downtown Baghdad, the Iraqis still had enough early warning radars in operation to see the tankers because we were refuelling only 45 miles south of the border. Once we had topped off our tanks, we had a strict time over target, which usually meant we would go straight there from the tanker. They could detect us while we were on the tanker, but when we broke off and completely stealthed up, we were invisible.

'During the first 48 hours of the war the Iraqi radar controllers must have figured out our target times, for all of a sudden, while we were lining our aim points up on the third night, all hell broke loose. They began firing everything they had straight up in the air. On earlier missions the firing didn't start until the first bombs exploded, so we knew they couldn't detect us.'

The first time this happened, the pilots reported it to their Intelligence people and a new tactic was devised – targeting Iraqi assets outside Baghdad. Sure enough, at the time when the Iraqis' assumed the F-117s were overhead the city, the sky lit up, yet no Nighthawks were in the area! Having proven that the Iraqis were using flight timings when it came to targeting the stealth fighters, the pilots of the 37th TFW(P) never again flew to Baghdad in a straight line. This in turn meant that their arrival times over their targets varied significantly, suitably confusing the Iraqi defenders. Some waves would hit targets within the city while others would concentrate on areas outside the capital.

In order to survive the nightly AAA firestorm over Baghdad, the Nighthawks had to remain unpredictable. Yet despite changing their tactics, the stealth pilots still had numerous close shaves due to the sheer amount of tracer being fired blindly into the night sky. Capt Mastny was amongst those to think that his number had come up during an early mission over Baghdad;

'There was no way to describe the intensity of the fire coming up from the ground. They had an endless supply of ammunition. One night I was more scared than on any of the others. I thought this was when I was going to be hit and have to bail out. Moments earlier, I had put my bombs on the targets, and I was now leaving the city with my throttle wide open.

'By leaning forward in the seat, you could get a pretty good view to the rear. As I was looking back over the sweep of my left wing, I saw the sky light up soon after my bombs had hit the target. There was AAA everywhere, and I could see these big white puffs and red ropes getting closer and closer. They were gaining on me every second, and were now only 25-30 ft off my wing. I believe the gunners were tracking me by the

The location of the most important targets outside Baghdad – the major IrAF airfields – are shown on this briefing slide, created by the 37th TFW post-war. These bases were systematically rendered inoperable, and the bulk of their state-of-the-art HASs destroyed, over a period of just a few days *(Rob Donaldson)*

sound of my engines – they were doing a very good job of it, but I doubt that they had radar-guided guns. They either caught a glimpse of my aircraft or were shooting at the sound. Just about the time I figured I was going to take one, I evidently went out of range, and it all drifted behind me. If they'd had bigger guns, I think they'd have nailed me.

'My biggest fear was not dying, but being captured. The enemy would have given anything to get their hands on an F-117 pilot. The flak I saw on that mission was just about every colour you could imagine – red, yellow, green and white.'

About two weeks after *Desert Storm* started, the 37th TFW's remaining squadron (the 417th TFTS) despatched six aircraft and several pilots from Tonopah to King Khalid to help ease the demanding workload of those already in-theatre. This aircraft was one of those sent to Saudi Arabia by the 417th TFTS *(Rose Reynolds)*

THE STRAIN BEGINS TO SHOW

Ten days into *Desert Storm*, the strain on the F-117 pilots was beginning to show. There was a continuing demand for their services because they had the night-precision capability that many other aircraft lacked, and they were invisible to any Iraqi radar still functioning. As the Nighthawk community was so small and the mission load so large, there were only two options open to the 37th TFW(P) – to bring in pilots from the wing's 417th TFTS or cut the workload. Obviously the latter was not acceptable, so the Tonopah-based training squadron was alerted for a move to King Khalid. Its CO, Lt Col Robert J Maher (Bandit No 308), described what happened next;

'Once the 416th had deployed, we were just about all that was left at Tonopah. We were told we wouldn't deploy under any circumstances because the continued training of stealth pilots couldn't be disrupted. When the war started, Lt Col L C Broline – my director of operations – moved over to manage our training programme while I went to the Command Post as one of the duty officers. Within a few days, I was notified by Col Klause to prepare for immediate deployment to the Middle East. The success rate achieved by the operational pilots, coupled with the long flight times involved, indicated that every possible pilot and aircraft would now have to be utilised in *Desert Storm*.

The KC-10 tankers in-theatre provided much of the fuel that in turn allowed F-117s to strike targets throughout Iraq *(Denny Lombard/Lockheed Martin)*

'At this time, our squadron's inventory was six F-117s and eight AT-38Bs. Staging through Langley as the others had done, we sent our Nighthawks on their way, supported by KC-10 tankers. We arrived on Day 10 of the war, and were soon integrated into the operational squadrons. The 417th didn't exist as a unit while deployed, and

my pilots flew with the other two squadrons. I spent most of my time in the command post, or supervising the combat mission planners or mission briefings.'

The instructors drafted in found the transition to frontline flying a relatively easy one to make thanks to the hard work they had put in readying themselves for just such a deployment whilst still at Tonopah. Attaining a combat edge whilst still in Nevada was one of Col Maher's key priorities when he assumed command of the unit in 1990;

Having completed his mission planning and pre-flight checks, Maj Jerry Sink (Bandit No 294) straps himself into his F-117 for another early evening mission. His jet is loaded with two 2000-lb GBU-10s, which were used against all manner of targets during *Desert Storm* (*Lockheed Martin*)

'When I took over the 417th TFTS, my main goal was to improve on the combat capabilities of my squadron's pilots. They were all excellent instructors, and I wanted them to be every bit as good as the guys who were flying in the operational units. Up to this point, our pilots would grab a mission folder from a pile that we kept and they would fly it to perfection. The problem was that they were hitting the same targets over and over, which provided very little training, or much of a challenge.

'Thanks to the significant efforts of Capts Ken Hoff (Bandit No 275) and Don Chapman (Bandit No 276), we began to gather target photos and flight plans from the operational guys, and we would fly these instead. This created an entirely new set of targets for us, and dramatically increased our training and proficiency. I also required both Hoff and Chapman to debrief together with the pilot they were training, and asked them to place a heavy emphasis on tape debriefing and bombing accuracy. Things soon became pretty competitive amongst pilots, as scores were kept for bombing accuracy.

'We were not in a combat zone during this training phase, but our leadership knew that we were ready if called upon.'

With the arrival of the instructors in-theatre, the F-117 pilots now typically only had to fly every other night, and spent their days off mission planning. More experienced personnel like Cols Whitley and Klause and Lt Col Maher flew every third night. That meant two of them would always be on the ground in case problems arose. Maher flew ten sorties

This close-up view of the aircraft seen above shows the all-important guidance units for the aircraft's GBU-10s. The jet carried the name *MEAN MIST* on its bomb-bay doors, but the exact identity of this F-117 remains unknown, as its name appears to have been changed prior to the Nighthawks returning to Tonopah (*Rose Reynolds*)

during his time at King Khalid, and when he returned from the last, he was greeted by 416th CO Lt Col Gonyea and the customary hosing down by his fellow pilots. He had been ordered back to Tonopah to supervise the training programme.

PROBLEM SOLVING

The F-117 wing enjoyed some stunning successes with its state-of-the-art weapon system that had never been tested under such

conditions. However, it also encountered the same sorts of problems as any other operational unit in-theatre, and had to solve them to avoid disrupting the nightly mission schedule. An example of improvisation that allowed the wing to remain effective occurred on the very first mission flown over Baghdad by 415th TFS weapons officer, Capt Marcel Kerdavid (Bandit No 284);

'My primary target was to be the tall Aquapark Communications Tower that resembled the Seattle Space Needle. When it came time to start engines, the right one in my jet simply would not work. I tried everything, and valuable time was slipping away. Fortunately, we had a spare jet set up, and when it became apparent that I wasn't going to get my primary aircraft started I jumped into the back-up F-117. I taxied out straight away and got airborne immediately in an effort to keep my all-important timings for refuelling and target attack as per the brief.

'There was only one thing wrong with the aircraft that I was now flying, and that was the fact that it was loaded with two GBU-27 LGBs. The bomb that I needed to knock out the tower was a GBU-10. This bothered me all the way to the target because the GBU-27 was a penetrator weapon that could easily punch right through the narrow tower and out the other side before it exploded. Our munitions experts had determined that the GBU-10, if well placed at the top of the tower, would explode on impact, destroying all the critical equipment that was positioned there. Regardless of the situation, I went with what I had.

'The tower was easy to locate, and as I got it in the cross-hairs, I dropped the bomb perfectly. I didn't hang around to observe the results because I had another target to hit. The next night, I was viewing the tape from another F-117 sortie that had taken out a target next to where the Aquapark Tower was and I was amazed! The tower was actually gone. What had happened was that the GBU-27 had hit perfectly, penetrating one side of the tower. Not having enough energy to go out the other side, the bomb dropped inside the tower, plummeting as its timed fuse was about to trigger the bomb. At a certain distance inside the tower, it exploded and the entire tower disintegrated. Strangely enough, the GBU-27 had worked better than the GBU-10 would have.

'The target had been the main communications facility in the centre of Baghdad. Jerry Leatherman (the 37th TFW(P)'s weapons officer) and I had worked long, hard hours drawing up the plans for this mission, and we sure didn't factor any mechanical problems into the equation!'

Until the results of these first F-117 missions were made public to the world, very few USAF personnel had understood the significance of this weapons system in the overall force make-up. That, of course, was partly due to the secrecy surrounding the project. Such ignorance meant that the results achieved during the war's first night had left senior Air Force commanders astounded. The latter also failed to grasp just how much preparatory work had been put into these first missions by the wing at King Khalid during *Desert Shield*, and this meant that they based their conclusions on the F-117's effectiveness as a weapon of war exclusively on the results of these well rehearsed strikes.

Within hours of *Desert Storm* commencing, Riyadh-based Intelligence, as well as agencies like the CIA, had begun to determine the future targets to be attacked. The image of infallibility that the F-117s had created during the first night of the war meant that 24 hours later, none of the 'urgent' targets were on the wing's hit list. Capt Leatherman described the frustration experienced during this period by planners and pilots alike;

'One of the greatest lessons learned during *Desert Storm* concerned our Intel community. They were great at gathering numbers and cold data, but they didn't talk to each other, and they would prioritise each target where it made sense from night to night. In fact, we took it upon ourselves to do our own bomb damage assessments because we weren't getting any reports from other agencies.

'Towards the middle part of the war, our wing became a "jack-of-all-trades". I remember one day when the Intel people called us and asked if we could bomb bridges. With our weapons people, we worked out that GBU-10s fitted with a very short delay in the fuse would be very effective in dropping bridges.'

BRIDGE-BUSTERS

US Marine Corps F/A-18 Hornet units had been ordered to destroy all the bridges in the Basra area in an effort to pin down Republican Guard troops in the city by cutting off the routes by which they could retreat. They did a good job despite heavy AAA, but with the Hornets mainly restricted to day-time operations, the 37th TFW(P) was told to attack the most heavily defended bridges at night. Capt Leatherman helped plan the strikes, and also led six F-117s to attack an identical number of key bridges in the southern Iraqi city of Basra, as well as Kuwait. He reported;

'We didn't miss any of them, but only four fell into the water. For a brief period we were bridge bombers! We went after bridges all over Iraq, including the most heavily defended ones within the city of Baghdad.'

Once again, the F-117 units found themselves at odds with Intelligence personnel over the right type of ordnance to use for this new mission. The success of the GBU-27 against deep bunkers and HASs led to an insistence that this weapon be used for attacks on the biggest bridges. The Nighthawk community believed the weapon was simply too large for the job, as although it would make a neat hole through the roadway part of the bridge, the bomb would invariably explode close to the water below, rendering the attack totally ineffective.

The GBU-27 was responsible for the destruction of most Iraqi HASs, which were often stuffed full of combat aircraft. This photograph was taken at Tallil after Coalition ground forces had moved through the area. Note that the HAS has had one of its heavy steel doors blown out when the bomb penetrated the concrete roof and then exploded *(Luke Atwell)*

When this was explained to Intelligence, it was then suggested to the F-117 pilots that they should aim their bombs at the cement pilings beneath the bridge, despite the fact that these would be impossible to detect from the air! The stealth pilots knew that it would only take one well-placed GBU-10 to render a bridge inoperable. They later proved their point by sending back pictures of the bridges that had been completely destroyed.

There was also some confusion over the way Iraqi HASs were to be hit, as Capt Leatherman explained;

37

'When the IrAF decided it didn't want to come out and play any more, our Intel discovered that it was hiding aircraft in newer HASs. They came to see us and asked if we could bomb them, so each night we would send six or eight pilots to certain airfields and take out two of the shelters each. We took out the first ones simultaneously, and then we would wander around in the general area out of hearing distance for 20-30 minutes in order to space the attack so the enemy had no idea if we were coming back. Then we'd go in and hit several more, dropping our remaining bombs at the same time, before heading back to the Saudi border.'

Intelligence wanted all the HASs knocked out as quickly as possible, so the same targets were also given to day fighter-bomber units. The 37th TFW(P), however, argued that this could be a waste of bombs, especially if the first attacks had already destroyed the target. The F-117 personnel had to explain to the planners in Riyadh that although satellite imagery might show that attacked HASs were still intact, they were not in fact. It was pointed out that the big penetration bomb used by the F-117s would make a small hole in the roof, but that as the LGB hit the floor of the shelter, it would explode, leaving a huge crater and gutting everything inside. On many occasions the doors were blown out, but this would not show up very well on the pictures seen by the planners at HQ.

Capt Leatherman knocked out his fair share of HASs, as he recalled;

'We would watch our own mission film so as to make a note of the HASs we had destroyed. We would mark them with an "X". Some airfields had 30 to 40 hardened shelters, so we only went after the ones we knew weren't hit by us. Intel didn't recognise what the GBU-27 penetrator could do, and they wouldn't list anything as destroyed unless it was laid to rubble as in World War 2 bombing photos – they just didn't know how these weapons worked. Our most effective bomb could be compared to a hollow point rifle bullet – where it enters the target isn't very impressive, but where it exits is!'

The F-111F-equipped 48th TFW, deployed from RAF Lakenheath to Taif RSAFB, formed an effective partnership with the 37th TFW(P)'s F-117s when it came to knocking out HASs. The swing-wing strike aircraft specialised in all-weather bombing from any altitude thanks to its Pave Tack laser designator system, which meant that the jet could employ LGBs with the same level of accuracy as the Nighthawk. However, the big F-111F was certainly not invisible to Iraqi radar.

Capt Rob Donaldson stands under a huge hole in one of Iraq's reinforced HASs at Tallil soon after the conflict had ended. These shelters were supposed to withstand virtually anything short of a nuclear blast, but clearly this one could not withstand the GBU-27's penetrating power *(Rob Donaldson)*

An F-117 taxis out to signal the start of yet another night of combat for the 37th TFW(P) from King Khalid. A visiting F-111F from the 48th TFW is visible in the background
(Rose Reynolds)

Although this photograph was taken on the eve of *Desert Storm*, this could just as easily be the scene after the F-117 had topped up its fuel tanks at the Saudi/Iraqi border, before setting course for Baghdad
(Lockheed Martin)

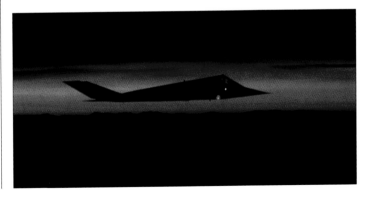

During *Desert Storm*, the F-111s flew 2500 sorties and were credited with more than 2200 confirmed hits on enemy targets. Many of the latter were HASs, as the F-111s shared in the destruction of the IrAF's numerous bases with the 37th TFW(P). This partnership was mentioned by Maj Rodney L Shrader when the author interviewed him;

'One of the best stories to come out of the war was our cooperation and coordination on various strikes with the F-111F guys. In the first 24 hours of the war, Iraqi fighters were in the air, and they got their butts whacked pretty badly by the F-15 Eagles (see *Osprey Combat Aircraft 53 - F-15C Eagle Units in Combat* for further details). This changed their strategy, and they stayed on the ground holed up in the shelters. I guess they figured we would let up, but they were wrong. At this point CENTAF decided to take out the enemy's air assets on the ground.

'One of the problems that we soon encountered following the commencement of this new offensive was the accuracy of the bomb damage assessments coming back to us from the CENTAF Intel folks. They wouldn't accept that video of a bomb entering a bunker or shelter proved that the target was destroyed. They had to have certain means of verification, and video just wasn't good enough for them.

'Often, we were sent against targets which we knew had already been destroyed. The F-111Fs were also sent against the same targets. So, to get the most "bang out of our bucks", we'd do some cross-coordination. We'd call the 48th TFW up and both of us would go carefully over the same map of the airfields. We would put an X on the bunkers they'd already hit and they'd put an X on the ones we'd taken out. So, when the "frag" (list of targets) came down and they wanted us to hit a shelter or bunker that had already been marked, we would change the target and go after one we knew was still intact. Good coordination like this allowed us to be more efficient in destroying the huge Iraqi war machine. Even though we were considered "loners", this proved we could work well with others.'

MISSION PLANNING

The F-117's 'invisibility' to Iraqi radar helped its pilots achieve an outstanding record during *Desert Storm*. And although the jet's stealthiness grabbed the headlines, there were many other factors behind this success whose crucial significance was known only to the pilots and mission planners. The best example of these hidden factors was the MPC. Each F-117 mission was meticulously planned down to the second by experienced personnel manning the MPC 24 hours a day.

One of their most important jobs was to plan entry and exit routes to and from the target, with these being determined by the presence of enemy SAM and AAA batteries and radar sites. It was only on very rare occasions that a mission route would follow a straight line.

When the 37th TFW(P) was deployed to the Middle East, one of the priority items to be loaded into the first C-5 transport that accompanied the F-117s was all the equipment needed to get the MPC up and running quickly. Among the key personnel involved in shifting the cell from Tonopah to King Khalid was the wing's senior electronic warfare officer, Maj Keith D Boyer. He and the other MPC staff had actually begun their long-term target planning on 2 August 1990 – just hours after news of the Iraqi invasion of Kuwait had broken. They continued their work right up to their departure for Saudi Arabia on 20 August. By that time they had planned attacks on major targets which were ready to be carried out as soon as the wing reached the Middle East.

This may sound a little premature, but for all the pilots and planners knew, their aircraft would be flying missions as soon as they arrived at King Khalid. Amongst the first targets highlighted for destruction were four sites located in and around the major airfield at Tallil. This base was singled out for treatment because of its close proximity to Saudi Arabia. A large force of Iraqi fighters was based there, and with a major communications centre nearby, it formed a vital cog in the air defence and communications network. In fact Tallil was the most important complex in the southeastern portion of Iraq – from the outskirts of Baghdad to the Kuwaiti border.

Maj Boyer recalled the pre-war planning process undertaken by the wing;

'By late October we had Night Two planned in detail, and 30 days later we had Night Three locked up. As we began working on Night Four, we were told that we would probably have to go back and hit some of the first three nights' targets again. This was because of the probability of near misses or of targets being only partially destroyed. Then we were told to back off on Night Three and not to worry about Night Four. As the time got closer, we were constantly hit with new Intel about the targets, and there were many changes that had to be made. It became an on-going change and upgrade situation.

'This was understandable because of the sheer quantity of military assets which Saddam had scattered all over Iraq. It was truly an armed fortress. By the first night of the war only a couple of targets survived all the changes made since September. As the enemy moved its defences around, it changed everything, and had a drastic ripple effect on the plan. If two aircraft were pulled off to handle other targets, some of which were much further away, it would change the sequence with the tankers. It all had to be reworked. Tanker rendezvous times, altitudes and sequences were strictly the responsibility of the mission planner-pilot types.'

Before the start of *Desert Storm*, Intelligence had determined that the city was ringed by about 60 SAM sites and 3000+ AAA emplacements. To put the threat posed to Coalition aircraft by these defences into perspective, it is a fact that during the Cold War the same number of SAM sites covered a huge area of the Warsaw Pact countries from northern East Germany down to southern Czechoslovakia. For any pilot whose aircraft was detected by radar, it would have been suicide to attempt a penetration of Baghdad's airspace. This demonstrates the difficulties and complications faced by the 37th TFW(P)'s MPC in plotting the safest routes to and from targets in this area.

Unlike the Vietnam War, when target selection was done from the White House, during *Desert Storm* this process was left to the military authorities in the field who had greater knowledge of the situation. But once the war started, it soon became clear that there were more targets than could realistically be attacked. While it was possible to track road traffic in and out of remote areas, which might indicate storage bunkers possibly containing chemical or nuclear stores, most turned out to be ammunition dumps, and there were more than could be counted. Maj Boyer added;

'We had to have accurate and up-to-date photography of the various target areas, as this imagery gave us the knowledge and ability, with our infrared targeting system, to consistently hit our aim points. We initially had problems getting the pictures we needed, however. Col Whitley went in to bat for us at command level, and after that we got exactly what we required until our tasking had ended.

'Despite the statements on television about our objectives for the first two nights of the war, Saddam Hussein made no attempt to bolster his defences around Baghdad. As a matter of fact, Intel stated that during the seven-year war with Iran, the latter attacked central Baghdad only twice. On the first occasion they didn't get a single bomb to fall within the city as all the attacking aircraft were shot down. When the second attack was made, two bombs were lobbed into Baghdad from a distance, and very little damage was done.

'The imagery we received from U-2 overflights and satellites was sufficient to give us the information we needed in order to put the cross-hairs on the crucial targets. The quality of these photographs was very good to the point that we could put a bomb down an air shaft or through a manhole cover. These shafts were the weak spots on top of reinforced buildings and bunkers.

After the F-117 had established its remarkable record in *Desert Storm*, US politicians were very keen to find out how it had been achieved. Here, Maj K D Boyer briefs US President George H W Bush and Secretary of the Air Force Donald B Rice. Maj Boyer was among the MPC personnel during the conflict *(K D Boyer)*

We had to be able to pick these out in the pictures so that our ordnance could successfully penetrate the target and destroy it.'

Faced with hitting such small target areas once the war started, the pilots of the 415th and 416th TFSs were thankful that there had been plenty of time to fly practice missions over the Saudi Arabian desert during *Desert Shield*. To complicate matters still further, the F-117 pilots had quickly found that targets in the Middle East appeared very differently on the infrared screens in their aircraft when compared with aim points regularly worked over in Nevada. Maj Shrader explained why;

'We began practising on just about every type of target you could imagine in that area. We had to get used to the IR signature of typical buildings in the southwest ranges we were flying over because the materials and method of construction used were different to back home, where we'd gained all our experience. Some buildings were made out of clay and stucco, and it was very difficult if you were asked to find a target in a small village as they all tended to blend into the background. Also, there was not much electricity used in some areas, thus reducing the number of heat sources emanating from target buildings on the Saudi ranges.

'We put in a lot of hours in the planning cell both before and during the war. Usually, the "frag" would come in at about 2200 hrs for the next day's missions. We'd work into the night and through the day so that everyone had their assignments in plenty of time to study them before the mission. This feat was achieved day after day thanks to the hard work put in by the members of the wing who participated in the planning sessions. Literally, there were thousands of missions "flown" in the MPC, but not

The key factor behind the Nighthawk's success in *Desert Storm* was mission planning. Members of the MPC at King Khalid got together for this group shot just days after the campaign had ended. Standing in the centre of the front row is Maj K D Boyer, who was the mission planning cell's senior EWO (*K D Boyer*)

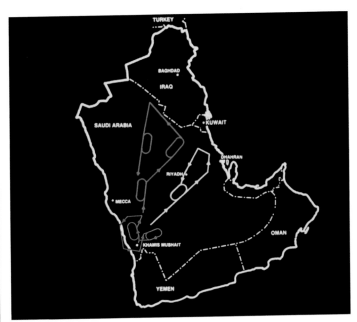

This USAF briefing diagram shows the designated air tanker tracks over Saudi Arabia during *Desert Storm* which were used by most strike aircraft participating in the air offensive. Note the F-117 base indicated in the lower left hand corner *(Rob Donaldson)*

Lt Col Greg Gonyea, 416th TFS CO, poses by his F-117A (86-0838, which was christened *MAGIC HAMMER*) prior to flying an early evening mission over Iraq in late February 1991. His Nighthawk logged a total of 36 missions during the air war *(Wes Cockman)*

nearly that many were actually flown by the F-117 force. We devised and reworked numerous plans based on what was sent down to us from Intel.'

Detailed planning of combat missions dates back to World War 2, although in those days successful missions over Germany and Japan involved hundreds of bombers. They carried unsophisticated 'dumb' bombs, and planners and pilots lacked computers.

By the 1990s, technology had advanced beyond anything that could have been imagined in the 1940s. Then, as during the F-117 missions of *Desert Storm*, timing was the key to success. Multi-ship attacks by Nighthawks took long hours of planning if they were to be executed perfectly, as 416th TFS CO Lt Col Greg Gonyea explained;

'Some very large targets were heavily defended and just one or two bombs couldn't do the job, so we worked on getting several of our jets over those targets at the same time for a simultaneous bomb release. Planners in the MPC started by putting a pair of aircraft over a single target such as a large building. The pilots would bomb either end of the structure, and this tactic worked so well that we started sending more aircraft against the same target. You just packed the F-117s in a little tighter. This way, we could put a large number of bombs in a small, concentrated area where a target complex consisted of several buildings grouped together.

'I'm not sure what the maximum number of aircraft sent over the same target was, but I know that it was quite a few. I've viewed a wartime video of stealth aircraft coming in, all in close proximity, with sets of bombs falling through the formations at timed intervals on the same target within seconds of each other – sheer precision, and all of this done at night! Ensuring the safety of our aircraft was the reason why this method of attack and delivery was initiated, as once the bombs hit, the AAA and SAMs immediately begin firing at random. But if the target was hit within a five- or six-second period, all the striking F-117s could be out of harm's way before the defensive fire erupted.'

Timing was indeed the critical factor, and all the necessary groundwork to achieve this was done in the MPC at King Khalid.

MEMORABLE MISSIONS

Considering the number of sorties assigned to the Nighthawk pilots during *Desert Storm*, it was surprising that the 37th TFW(P) was not continually running out of bombs. On some nights, three waves of F-117s were launched, which meant that the aircraft flew at least once, and some of them twice – each jet carried two Paveway II/III LGBs. Their attacks were so accurate, and so effective, that they would knock out a target with just a solitary bomb, before heading elsewhere and destroying a second target with similar accuracy. However, both bombs would have to be dropped on the same target if it was heavily fortified.

The GBU-10 Paveway II and GBU-27 Paveway III were the weapons most widely used by the F-117s. Both were 2000-lb LGBs, and the latter bomb was used exclusively by the F-117. Indeed, the GBU-27 proved itself to be so effective that the USAF labelled it the top penetration weapon used in *Desert Storm*. It was cloaked in secrecy until the war started, with the stealth pilots having only been introduced to it in the early days of the conflict. Most of the wing's weapons specialists were also unfamiliar with the LGB, but they learned quickly, and it was ready for deployment by 17 January 1991. Without the GBU-27, most Iraqi HASs would have remained intact.

When viewing the GBU-10 and -27 side by side, it is difficult to tell them apart except for the fact that the latter weapon's guidance head is bigger and its nose fins clipped to allow the LGB to fit in the F-117's snug bomb-bay. Aircraft typically carried two bombs of the same type in their bays, although the load could occasionally consist of a single example of each LGB.

As the war progressed, and the 37th TFW(P)'s appetite for GBU-10/27s showed no sign of abating, the demand for these bombs proved to be so great that the wing occasionally had to resort to using the more common 500-lb GBU-12. Because of its smaller size, this weapon was only effective against certain targets. The shortage of GBU-10/27s arose so suddenly that C-5 transports had to be hastily despatched to Kunsan AB, in South Korea, and RAF Mildenhall, in England, to fetch more bombs from stockpiles held near to both bases.

In the war's early stages, CENTAF planning staff were not only selecting the next day's targets, but also designating the weapons to be used. However, the F-117 pilots soon became responsible for their own weapon selection following poor results from early attacks on HASs. Amongst the first examples targeted were the 39 shelters located at the Balad South-East airfield complex some 50 miles north of Baghdad. With its two 11,000-ft runways, this base represented one of the highest

priority targets in Iraq outside the capital, and as the IrAF was known to have about 800 fighters, Balad probably housed more aircraft than any other airfield. Wing CO Col Whitley recalled the attacks on this target;

'The two missions I remember most were flown against the same target – Balad airfield. Early in the conflict we were directed against a large number of HASs in an effort to eliminate Iraqi interceptors. Because these airfields were heavily defended, the task was given to the F-117s. But we had the wrong weapons on board. We were tasked with attacking these targets with 2000-lb blast-fragmentation bombs which had a nose plug and a delayed tail fuse. Although we vehemently objected to the weapons selection by the CENTAF planning staff, we were told to execute the order as it had come down, which we did. The results were pitiful against these heavily defended targets.

'Although the weapons people built and loaded the bombs as directed, and we flew the missions exactly as planned, the results were miserable despite outstanding accuracy. In almost every case the bombs simply exploded on the exterior of the shelters, causing little damage to the structures or contents.

'While the explosions made for some impressive video, the pilots weren't happy about being exposed to stiff ground defences for so little result. We learned a lesson from this, and subsequently fought battles with the planning staff to ensure that our weapons system was being employed in the most appropriate manner. Bomb selection for this target had nothing to do with the lack of understanding of the F-117. It was a breakdown in "the system" which led to a waste of some very valuable combat sorties.'

Col Al Whitley taxies out for another night mission in aircraft 85-0813 *THE TOXIC AVENGER*, which had already flown 29 missions by the time this photograph was taken – it would complete 35 by war's end. That meant that the jet was in the air virtually every night during *Desert Storm*, although not always with Col Whitley at the controls *(Eric Schulzinger/Lockheed Martin)*

This shot was taken in the late afternoon at King Khalid, by which time the pilots involved in the first wave of missions had finished their briefings and commenced their launch countdowns. Here, an F-117 pilot prepares to start his engines. Many more LGB silhouettes would be added to this aircraft's mission tally by war's end *(Rose Reynolds)*

This still, taken from the target video camera fitted to an F-117, appears to show a HAS which has been penetrated by a GBU-27 LGB. In some cases the heavy steel doors of these hangars were blown out by the exploding bombs as if they were made of plywood *(Lockheed Martin)*

Many of the pilots involved in this first Balad mission commented on the frustration they felt at having to return to this target. Capt Michael D Riehl (Bandit No 320) was among them;

'That flight to Balad South-East was memorable because the F-111Fs had tried to take it out during the day and had had to turn back because there was so much AAA. We had already attacked other airfields with great success, so we were put up for this one too. Most of the revetments at those other airfields looked like A-frames with the top chopped off (very hard) or like concrete Quonset Huts (fairly soft). When we received photos of the Balad revetments, they looked like something that was going to be very hard to crack. When the "frag" arrived from Riyadh, I immediately noticed that they'd assigned GBU-10s to knock the HASs out. I went to our weapons officer and told him that I thought we should use the GBU-27s instead. However, he assured me that a GBU-10 would do the job. To make it more effective we added a nose plug instead of a nose fuse. The rest of the mission planning was normal.

'We planned for our aircraft to hit the revetments, then do a timing loop and come back to hit another shelter, before heading back to the border. To help us beat the AAA we planned our attack at a medium altitude, and when we flew the mission it all started pretty well.'

Evidently, the Iraqi gunners had been expecting an attack from a much lower altitude, for most of their rounds burst far below the F-117s, although the heavier 57 mm shells were fused to explode far above the aircraft. Capt Riehl's first bomb had a faulty guidance system which prevented him from hitting his target, so he immediately flew a timing loop and came back for another attempt. His second GBU-10 struck the target dead centre, but instead of seeing a hole in the HAS's roof and an explosion that blew its doors off, all he saw was a giant smoke ring. It was clear that the target remained intact.

Riehl's first reaction was that both his bombs had been faulty. However, once back at King Khalid, other pilots made similar comments. Balad South-East would have to be attacked once again.

Ultimately, and most unexpectedly, the use of ineffective GBU-10s against the HASs was to have a posi-

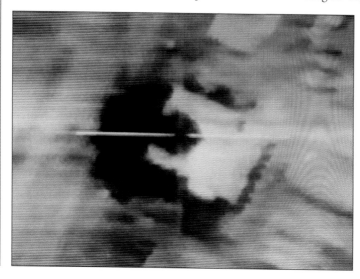

tive outcome. Because the first wave of bombs could not penetrate the shelters, the IrAF were fooled into thinking that they were safe to use. As a result, they moved a significant number of aircraft from scattered positions on the airfield into what they believed was the safety of bomb-proof shelters. But the F-117 pilots returned with GBU-27s fitted with hardened penetration heads and duly had a field day – all 39 HASs were destroyed, along with the aircraft jammed inside them. The AAA was as heavy as

before, but the pilots claimed it had been worth the risk. Capt Riehl also participated in the second Balad mission;

'Apparently, the Iraqis were convinced that their new shelters were far better than any of our ordnance. Our Intelligence sources at Riyadh confirmed that Saddam Hussein's pilots were moving a large number of aircraft from scattered airfields into Balad South-East because of these "bomb proof" shelters. It didn't take long for us to be tasked with further attacks, but this time we weren't questioned about the ordnance we should carry – it would definitely be the GBU-27s. We went back and levelled them all, and none were empty. This mission sent the IrAF into a state of panic, and shortly afterwards Iraqi jets began fleeing to Iran. They were met by a swarm of F-15 Eagles, and the latter shot down as many as they could catch in the air.'

When the Nighthawks attacked the HASs at Balad South-East airfield, they were ordered to use GBU-10s (seen here), but these weapons failed to penetrate the shelters. When they returned for another attack, the F-117s carried GBU-27 deep penetration weapons, which destroyed the hangars and their contents (Rose Reynolds)

Maj Jeff Moore's F-117 awaits its pilot for another night strike. Most maintenance and weapons tasks were performed inside HASs at King Khalid (Rose Reynolds)

BAD WEATHER

Most missions flown by the Nighthawks were tense and lengthy ones. Many pilots stated that they could only relax once they had crossed back into Saudi Arabia, had topped up from the tanker and were heading south to King Khalid. One of the major causes for concern was the weather over Iraq during January and February 1991. If the altitude for an attack was low enough to force the F-117 below cloud, then the aircraft could easily be spotted with the naked eye on the ground. Conversely, if a pilot found himself in cloud over the target then he could not use his FLIR/DLIR to see his aim point. A change in altitude was also strictly forbidden unless it had been planned, as most missions were simultaneous multi-ship attacks, where a switch in height greatly increased the risk of a mid-air collision.

Some pilots took advantage of what they described as a lucky break in the weather at the last second over the target. One was Capt Riehl who flew two missions to the H-2 and H-3 airfield complexes;

'The mission was pretty standard – ingress according to the mission plan, attack one airfield, hit a couple of timing points, attack the second airfield and then back home. When I got on the route and over the first target, I was totally in the "soup". The only things I could see were the tracers coming up through the clouds. I imagine they didn't like the sound of us flying over their airfield! All of a sudden I popped out of the cloud with about 30 seconds to go until I dropped my bomb. Luckily, the aeroplane was all armed up and had the world's best INS (Inertial Navigation System). The cursor was sitting right on top of the target. I dropped the bomb and guided it, wondering how long the weather would hold. The second I saw the bomb impact the shelter, I popped right back into the clouds and was on my way out of there.'

Very few missiles were fired after the third night of the war because most of the enemy radar had been knocked out. AAA remained a threat throughout the campaign, however, and with the F-117s forced down to lower altitudes in order to achieve the increased impact angles required for the successful employment of the GBU-27 against hardened targets, smaller-calibre weapons could now also bracket the aircraft. Capt Jeffrey Moore (Bandit No 292) recalled;

'Our primary penetration weapon was the GBU-27, and it had a pitch-down delivery profile. The latter increased the impact angle, but forced a lower delivery altitude. To gain a higher altitude capability, we could have the weapon loaders lock out the pitch-down profile. The only problem was that the delivery avionics still expected a standard GBU-27 profile. If the bomb information was loaded into the MFDs (multi-functional displays) it would programme release and guidance cues for a standard pitch-down profile.'

The GBU-27 was designed for operations involving low altitude, high-speed delivery. The standard GBU-27 delivery profile was a short ballistic drop followed by a hard pitch almost vertically downwards. At that point the guidance equipment started flying the weapon along the laser beam 'painted' by the aircraft. This allowed an F-117 to deliver its bomb from low altitude, as the weapon could achieve a near vertical impact on the target, with the aircraft still maintaining laser energy on the aim point.

Without the all-important pitch-down manoeuvre from low altitude, unacceptably low impact angles would result – in such strikes it was feared that the GBU-27 would lack sufficient inertia to penetrate its hardened target. But this standard pitch-down profile only worked from relatively low altitudes, for the gimbal limit of the DLIR was reached before the weapon's impact on longer time-of-flight profiles at medium and high altitudes. Capt Moore explained;

'Along comes *Desert Storm* and we don't need low altitude delivery any more. Now we want medium and high altitude capabilities. We still want the superior penetration of the GBU-27 and the improved kill probability associated with the proportional guidance kit. Besides, we don't have many GBU-10/12s, but we have plenty of GBU-27s, and we don't want to drive ourselves down to the high risk, low altitude arena just to achieve acceptable weapons effects.

'What we needed was a way of turning off the standard GBU-27's pitch-down manoeuvre and tricking the F-117's delivery computer into providing an optimal ballistic weapons release point. Luckily, the GBU-27's guidance kit allowed us to eliminate the pitch-down phase of the standard delivery mode. Now all we needed was a way of tricking the weapons delivery computer into providing an optimal release point for a free-fall GBU-27, rather than one being targeted via a pitch-down delivery (*text continues on page 62*).

COLOUR PLATES

1
F-117A 81-10796 *FATAL ATTRACTION*, assigned to Capt Daniel DeCamp, 415th TFS/37th TFW(P), King Khalid RSAFB, January 1991

2
F-117A 81-10798 *ACES AND EIGHTS*, assigned to Maj Joseph Bouley, 415th TFS/37th TFW(P), King Khalid RSAFB, February 1991

49

3

F-117A 82-0803 *UNEXPECTED GUEST*, assigned to Capt Scott Stimpert, 416th TFS/37th TFW(P), King Khalid RSAFB, February 1991

4

F-117A 83-0807 *THE CHICKENHAWK*, assigned to Maj Steve Edgar, 415th TFS/37th TFW(P), King Khalid RSAFB, January 1991

5

F-117A 84-0810 *DARK ANGEL*, assigned to Maj Jon Boyd, 416th TFS/37th TFW(P), King Khalid RSAFB, February 1991

6

F-117A 84-0812 *Axel*, assigned to Capt Brian Foley, 415th TFS/37th TFW(P), King Khalid RSAFB, February 1991

7
F-117A 85-0813 *THE TOXIC AVENGER*, assigned to Col Alton Whitley, 37th TFW(P), King Khalid RSAFB, February 1991

8
F-117A 85-0814 *FINAL VERDICT*, assigned to Capt Kenneth Huff, 416th TFS/37th TFW(P), King Khalid RSAFB, February 1991

9

F-117A 85-0816 *LONE WOLF*, assigned to Maj Gregory A Feest, 415th TFS/37th TFW(P), King Khalid RSAFB, January 1991

10

F-117A 85-0818 *The Overachiever*, assigned to Lt Col Barry E Horne, 415th TFS/37th TFW(P), King Khalid RSAFB, January 1991

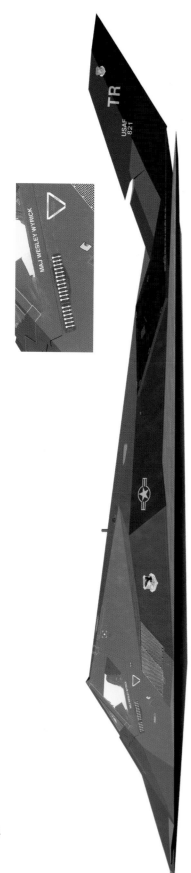

11
F-117A 86-0821 *SNEAK ATTACK*, assigned to Maj Wesley Wyrick, 415th TFS/37th TFW(P), King Khalid RSAFB, February 1991

12
F-117A 84-0825 *"MAD-MAX"*, assigned to Lt Col Ralph Getchell, 415th TFS/37th TFW(P), King Khalid RSAFB, February 1991

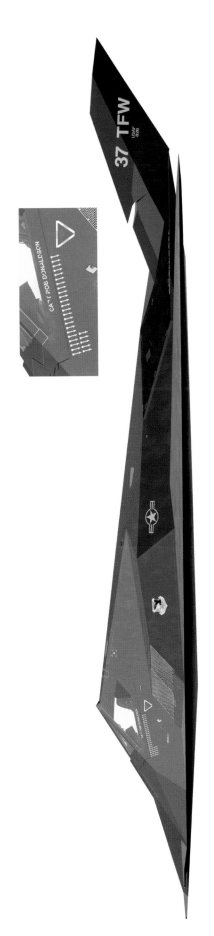

13

F-117A 84-0826 *NACHTFALKE*, assigned to Capt Rob Donaldson, 415th TFS/37th TFW(P), King Khalid RSAFB, February 1991

14

F-117A 85-0830 *BLACK ASSASSIN*, assigned to Maj Robert D Eskridge, 416th TFS/37th TFW(P), King Khalid RSAFB, February 1991

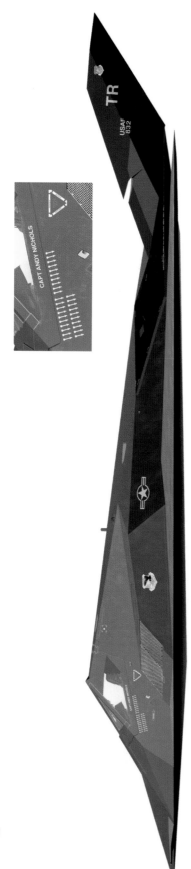

15
F-117A 85-0832 *ONCE BITTEN*, assigned to Capt Andy Nichols, 416th TFS/37th TFW(P), King Khalid RSAFB, February 1991

16
F-117A 85-0834 *NECROMANCER*, assigned to Maj Jeffrey Moore, 416th TFS/37th TFW(P), King Khalid RSAFB, February 1991

17
F-117A 86-0837 *HABU II*, assigned to Capt Matthew Byrd, 416th TFS/37th TFW(P), King Khalid RSAFB, February 1991

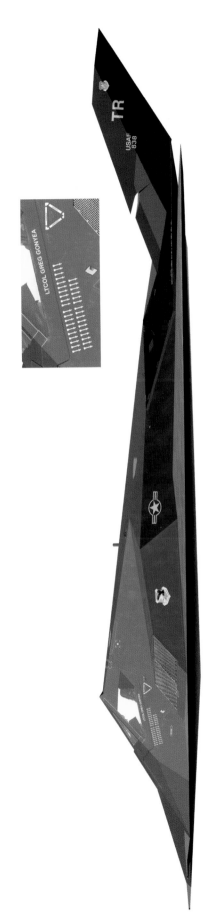

18
F-117A 86-0838 *MAGIC HAMMER*, assigned to Lt Col Greg Gonyea, 416th TFS/37th TFW(P), King Khalid RSAFB, February 1991

19
F-117A 86-0839 *MIDNIGHT REAPER*, assigned to Maj Joseph Salata, 415th TFS/37th TFW(P), King Khalid RSAFB, February 1991

20
F-117A 88-0841 *Mystic Warrior*, assigned to Maj Rod Shrader, 416th TFS/37th TFW(P), King Khalid RSAFB, January 1991

21
F-117A 88-0842 *IT'S HAMMERTIME*, assigned to Capt Richard Cline, 416th TFS/37th TFW(P), King Khalid RSAFB, February 1991

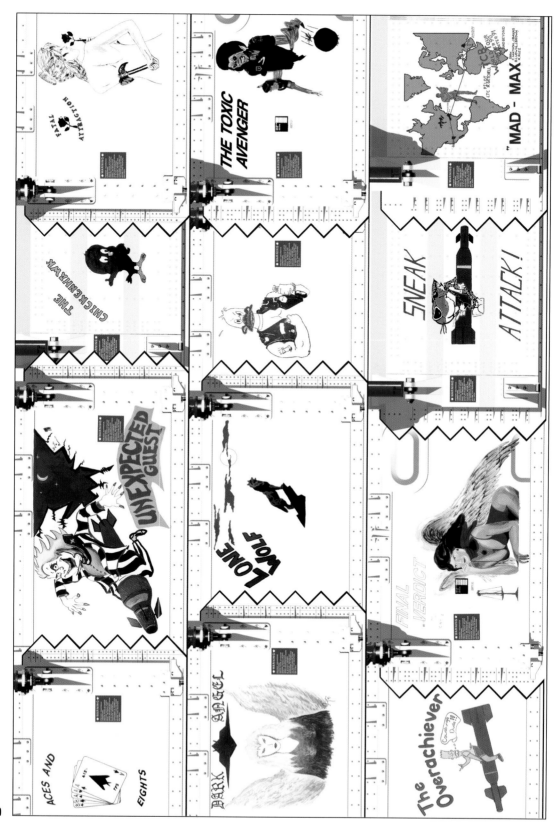

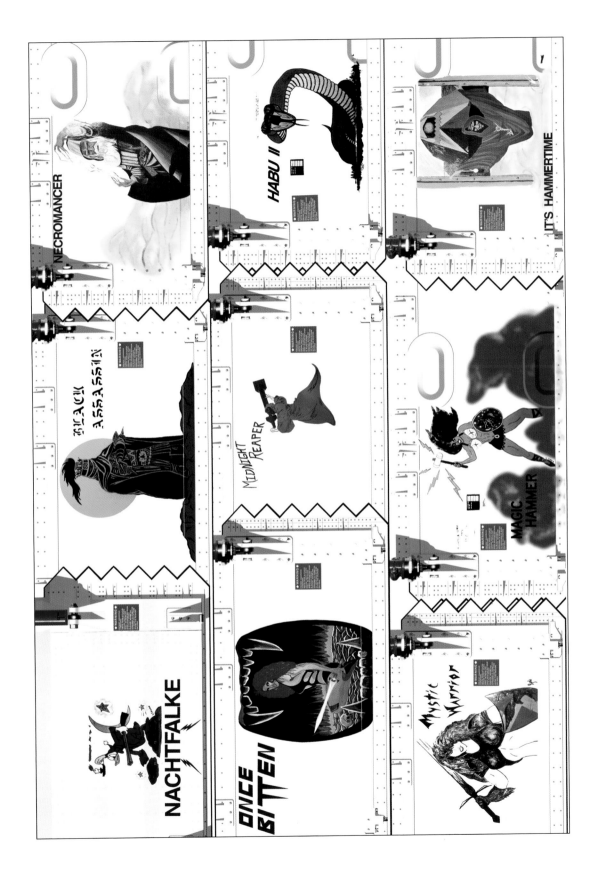

NECROMANCER

HABU II

IT'S HAMMERTIME

BLACK ASSASSIN

MIDNIGHT REAPER

MAGIC HAMMER

NACHTFALKE

ONCE BITTEN

MYSTIC WARRIOR

61

'I put together a quick request with squadron CO, Lt Col Gonyea, to fly a test profile with the GBU-27 which had the guidance kit manually locked out of the pitch-down profile and the GBU-12 information loaded on the MFDs. This would give GBU-12 delivery and guidance cues, but with a ballistic trajectory for the GBU-27. The perfect test target, I offered, would be a HAS. It could be hit 45 degrees from vertical and still impact the sloped surface of the shelter at about 90 degrees.'

Capt Moore would get to test the modified GBU-27 during one of the first multi-aircraft airfield attacks made by the 37th TFW(P). These strikes required precise timing, with slight altitude separation, and the tactics employed were used more against the huge H-2 and H-3 airfield complexes than on any other single target in *Desert Storm*. Such attacks sometimes called for two waves of F-117s, with one hitting H-2 and the other H-3. Then they would loop around, crossing paths, before repeating the process on the opposite airfield. These tactics worked to perfection, indicating the effectiveness of the pilots' training.

Capt Moore was one of those involved in the development of this tactic, and he explained to the author how he tested his modified GBU-27 delivery profile during a multi-aircraft attack on H-2 and H-3;

'My wish was granted for the test delivery to take place during one of the first multi-ship simultaneous impact missions to be sent against H-2 and H-3. I flew the mission in my GBU-27-equipped F-117 with GBU-12 MFD information downloaded into its delivery computer, and the 415th TFS sortied a similarly armed aircraft with GBU-10 MFD information for comparative purposes.

'My mission profile took me over H-3 first. I'd planned my delivery to take place just before the other aircraft – using the normal low, pitch-down profile – so I'd have good target acquisition before their weapons impacted. Since my bomb's time of flight was considerably longer due to it being released at a greater height, it allowed the other F-117s to clear the area before it came through their altitude. My release profile also meant that I could target the bomb more accurately thanks to the elimination of the infrared picture distortion associated with the weapon impacts from my wingmates. The latter had totally cleared by the time I started the final guidance phase of the profile.

Once preparations for the F-117s involved in the first wave of attacks had been completed, the jets were usually lined up on the ramp at King Khalid so that maintainers could get to second wave jets in the HASs more easily. Here, the pilots have strapped into these Nighthawks and started their engines, prior to taxiing out at the pre-briefed time *(Rose Reynolds)*

Right
The maintenance crews and weapons specialists worked almost non-stop from the time the last F-117 returned from a mission just before dawn until the next launch the following sunset. The 2000-lb GBU-27s seen in this shot were the weapons normally used in attacks against hardened targets in Iraq. These bombs are being prepared for fusing by armourers from the 37th TFW(P) *(Rose Reynolds)*

'The AAA was enormous, and the most southerly airfield was a bust because of the weather over the target. But the aircraft hitting the extreme northwest corner of the complex had it a little better because the cloud cover there was thin.'

When they arrived over the second airfield, the F-117s met a AAA barrage that was just as intense as that encountered over the first target. However, the weather was better. Capt Moore continued;

'I got target acquisition and weapons release right on time. In one corner of my HAS target I noted a circular AAA revetment with what I think was a 23 mm gunner doing his best to burn his barrel out. Moments after I released, as if on cue, the IR picture distorted from the impact of the bombs from other F-117s in the immediate vicinity. When the picture returned, I mentally noted the lack of ground fire from that particular gun pit.

Above
The F-117 seen in the background of this photograph has just returned from a pre-dawn mission. Once refuelled, it will be towed into its HAS for routine maintenance and rearming with two of the GBU-27s seen on the bomb trolley in the foreground (Wes Cockman)

'My bomb hit fine and "spluged" the target – "spluge" was a term we coined for the devastating effect rendered on the DLIR when a HAS that had been stuffed with more than one fully-fuelled aircraft was hit. There must have been at least three fully-fuelled jets crammed into this particular shelter. The seams of the shelter literally erupted and split apart. It was a spectacular display of over-pressure acting on something slightly less than immovable.

'Needless to say, the test was very successful. Thereafter, the majority of our GBU-27 deliveries were done using this "trick the system" profile,

unless a specific weapons effect was needed for a target which could only be achieved by a near-vertical impact. When I reviewed my tape after the mission, the weapon hit on the HAS next to mine resulted in one of the big steel entry doors coming unhinged. I could see the door flipping almost effortlessly into my DLIR field of view as the IR distortion subsided. It flew right into the AAA pit which I'd noted before my bomb release. I had to stop-frame review that hit several times with the guy who had delivered the bomb

(Capt Scott Stimpert, Bandit No 270). He shacked the HAS with his GBU-27 and the gunner with the shelter door – a double kill.'

TALLIL STRIKE

Another spectacular HAS mission against the airfield at Tallil was flown on the night of 8 February, and this again offered further testimony to the GBU-27's destructive power. Although the base had been attacked on several previous occasions by F-117s, reconnaissance photos of the airfield revealed that there were still several shelters that appeared to be unscathed. Capt Joseph A Salata (Bandit No 295), who was flying aircraft 86-0839 *MIDNIGHT REAPER*, remembered how the attack unfolded;

'The Tallil complex AAA was always heavy. Even though we'd flown against it many times before, it was still a dangerous target. There were so many HASs scattered around the area that we had to go back and finish off the remaining ones. On this day, we had a chance to do just that. A combined attack of several types of conventional night precision droppers preceded us, and we sent about a dozen Nighthawks to take out what was left. I was in the last aircraft in the strike package. I could see the devastation caused by the jets which had already dropped their loads.

'On my first pass, I dropped a 2000-lb GBU-27 right through the eastern half of a double shelter. During the pass, I noticed the shape of what appeared to be a Russian-built "Hind" helicopter parked outside the remaining half of my target. Our Intel had discovered that the Iraqis were removing some of the aircraft from the HAS and parking them out in the open in the hope that they might survive. On my next pass, I aimed my remaining bomb at the intact portion of my original target. I tried to make it impact as close to the "Hind" as possible. When the bomb exploded inside the shelter, the overpressure blew out the heavy multi-ton steel door, crushing the helicopter in the process.

'Right after the war, Coalition damage assessment teams visited the remains of that particular HAS and found the charred wreckage of a

Mission recently completed, a last wave jet is towed back into its HAS for maintenance. A small team of specialist groundcrew would have 16-18 hours to get this F-117 turned around ready for its next foray into Iraq the following night *(Rose Reynolds)*

This state-of-the-art HAS at Tallil was reduced to rubble in seconds, along with its contents, when a GBU-27 penetrated its steel-reinforced concrete roof. Note that the doors have been blown out. An IrAF Mi-8 that was parked near the HAS also appears to have been destroyed by flying debris *(Luke Atwell)*

destroyed MiG-25 inside. I ended up with my two bombs destroying both shelters and two aircraft.'

Another 415th TFS pilot who flew numerous missions against HASs was Capt Robert Donaldson, whose father had flown fast jets during the Vietnam War. His recollections of his first mission in a later conflict, and the hours leading up to it, are very clear;

'Late in the afternoon of 16 January, we were told to eat a good meal and come to the aircraft shelter, where our briefings were conducted. Our CO, Col Whitley, quickly informed us that this was it – we're taking it to them tonight. The atmosphere was very calm, professional and business-like – this was exactly what we'd been training for. All of us were ready to go right then, especially those of us who had been in Saudi Arabia since August.

'We took off in two-ship elements and did a "comm-out" (no communications) rendezvous with the tanker. Everything was done on timing – at this time you start engines, at this time you taxi out of your shelter area, at this time you meet up with the other aircraft in your element and so on. This was done every night for each wave, and there was no communication whatsoever.

'We took off in pairs, and the first attack wave consisted of 20 F-117s. We met ten tankers from Riyadh and all aerial refuelling was done in total radio silence. We split up at the border for our individually-assigned targets. The first bombs were dropped near the Saudi-Iraq border area by Maj Greg A Feest and his wingman. The overall plan for the first wave was to blast a hole along the border to ensure that non-stealthy aircraft could get through safely.'

As detailed in the previous chapter, Maj Feest was briefed to hit airfields in southwest Iraq so as to reduce Saddam Hussein's chances of launching 'Scud' surface-to-surface ballistic missiles against Israel. Feest's element also destroyed the Interceptor Operations Centre from which Iraqi interceptors and 'Scuds' were controlled. The coordination between his element and the other aircraft in the wave was a study in perfection. Minutes after Feest's element had taken out their targets, the remaining Nighthawks commenced their destruction of downtown Baghdad.

65

Capt Rob Donaldson checks every detail of his aircraft's performance with his crew chief after a night mission over Baghdad. The maintenance personnel put in long hours to keep these aircraft in the air virtually every night *(Rob Donaldson)*

Although the F-117s were subsonic aircraft, they always made their attacks on targets heavily defended by AAA at full throttle. On some missions they had difficulty returning to friendly airspace before first light because of bad weather in the target areas *(Rose Reynolds)*

On that first night of the war, F-117s ranged as far south as Tallil airfield, which was an important interceptor coordination centre covering Iraq's extreme southern sector. The purpose of such a precision attack was to completely blind the enemy on a wide front, thus preventing the Iraqis from detecting the non-stealthy aircraft that were following in the F-117s' wake. Capt Donaldson continued;

'The aerial campaign of *Desert Storm* systematically rolled back the Iraqi defences. Once the first bomb was dropped, they started firing everything they had into the air. Some of their radar units were still up, and they could see the A-6s, F-111s, tankers etc. on their screens. They were relaying all this information to Baghdad.

'The F-117s which followed the lead element over the city were met by a firestorm of AAA and SAMs, but they were shooting blindly. They weren't able to get any radar locks or visuals on anything that was up over the city. We never received so much as a scratch. As we flew through all of this, you could see the intermittent explosions of bombs from the aircraft in front of us.'

The mission Capt Donaldson recalled most vividly was when he hit a bridge in the Basra area;

'This mission was flown well into the war, just as Iraqi troops started retreating out of Kuwait. Our command wanted to drop all the bridges across the rivers and marshes so that Saddam couldn't safely evacuate his army and equipment. I put a GBU-10 dead centre on a bridge, which dropped the entire span. A truck was racing across at the time. It was all caught on film. Capt Salata dropped a huge bridge into the water using a single GBU-10. You could compare this feat to World War 2, when

scores of bombers were assigned to attack a large bridge in Europe. It was a spectacular sight because the entire structure dropped in one piece. It was so big that it resembled the Golden Gate Bridge!'

Capt Joseph Salata remembered this target too;

'That mission took place on 9 February – the night after I'd blown out the door of a HAS and destroyed the "Hind" helicopter with the same bomb. We had been sent out to destroy the July 14th Memorial Bridge. Maj Jerry Leatherman had hit it several minutes before I dropped my LGB.

'In preparation for the mission, both of us studied the reconnaissance photos and noticed that our target was a suspension bridge. We decided that in order to inflict as much damage on it as possible, we'd have to place a bomb right on top of one of the supports. We'd also been warned during the weather briefing that the winds around Basra were going to be extremely strong. On the run-in heading that we were going to use, the wind was going to be off our nose from the left.

'Maj Leatherman stated that he would aim for the top-centre of the near support and I would have to judge my aim point off his bomb impact. As I approached the bridge, I noticed that his bomb had missed slightly to the right due to the heavy winds. In fact, it looked almost like someone had taken a bite out of the right side of the support. For an instant, nothing happened after my LGB hit the support. I thought I hadn't caused much damage. Suddenly, the entire bridge started moving downwards. In a matter of seconds it had hit the water, causing a massive splash on both sides of the river. It was spectacular, and I remember how anxious I was to get back to King Khalid to show the video to the rest of the guys.'

This stealth fighter is returning to King Khalid from an early morning mission over enemy territory. Because of the distance of their Saudi bases from the border with Iraq, the missions flown by F-117 pilots normally lasted five to six hours *(Rose Reynolds)*

Rolled out of its hangar, this aircraft has its GBU-10s exposed so that the pilot can pre-flight check them prior to declaring the F-117 mission ready *(Ken Huff)*

HIGH WORK LOAD

Throughout *Desert Storm*, the 37th TFW(P) would typically launch two or three waves of F-117s per night from King Khalid, with each wave averaging a dozen or more air-craft. The first wave would usually depart at 1730 hrs and recover at 2200 hrs. The second wave would take-off before the first had landed, putting them over their targets at between 0030 and 0100 hrs. The third, and final, wave, which occa-sionally included some pilots who had participated in the first wave, usually took off at about 0200 hrs

and arrived over their targets at 0430 hrs. Thanks to the campaign being fought in the height of the winter time in the Middle East, the nights were at their longest at this time of year, allowing jets from the last wave to recover at first light.

This intense work load soon led to pilots becoming exhausted, and the situation was only eased by the arrival of still more aircrew from the 417th TFTS.

The 416th's Capt Scott Stimpert had been sent to Saudi Arabia with the second deployment during *Desert Shield*, and his recollections of that period graphically indicate the difficulty of executing all the strike orders pouring out of Riyadh;

'Working in the MPC made it more complicated because a typical sortie might take off at 1730 hrs, returning to base at about 2300 hrs, then go straight into the cell for 12 to 14 hours, planning the next night's three waves of strikes. After that, we'd try to get eight hours sleep, before take-off at 2200 hrs and recovery at about 0300 hrs. It was a frenzied pace that made it difficult to determine just how many days had passed between missions.'

An event that Stimpert was to remember vividly occurred on 26 January during one of the first coordinated airfield attacks. He recalled;

'We launched eight aircraft for this particular attack on H-2 and H-3. Four of our aircraft were to fly over H-2 and the other four were to hit H-3 all at the same time, with simultaneous time-over-target (TOT). Then we had to fly north, cross with one set flying counter-clockwise, pass to the right and hit the airfields again with our one remaining bomb. After that, we would all head for the border and recover back at King Khalid. Although you had four aircraft over the same target at the same time, all were at separate altitudes and had differing TOTs. So it was a coordinated single-ship attack rather than a four-ship one such as might have been executed by F-15Es or F-16s.'

Capt Stimpert and the other seven stealth pilots hit their first targets, and there was less AAA fire than expected. Each aircraft was loaded with GBU-27s and, at that stage of the war, no one was sure if they were actually penetrating the HASs and destroying their contents. However, reconnaissance photos would soon confirm the bomb's accuracy and destructive ability – it performed exactly as its nickname 'Bunker Buster' suggested. The foreign-built HASs, thick with steel and concrete, ultimately proved to be no match for the weapon. Capt Stimpert continued;

'We attacked the first airfield at H-2, and right after we dropped our first bombs I glanced towards H-3. I could see a bright flash that looked like a small nuclear explosion. It was a huge secondary detonation, and I didn't think much more about it, as I was concentrating on what I was doing. I was flying north of H-2, crossing in the dark with the other four F-117s, and initiating my attack approach to the other airfield.

'Digressing just a bit at this point, we would use three photographs to work up our attack profiles prior to flying the mission – we would then take these images with us in the cockpit. One of these photos would be an overall shot of the area being targeted. The second image was from medium range, whilst the third was a close-up of the actual target the bomb was to hit. When it was a HAS or a taxiway, you'd have to do a counting exercise like "okay, my target is the fourth shelter from the main taxiway". You'd match your pictures with what you were seeing on your FLIR/DLIR. So there I was, sitting over the airfield looking for my HAS, which was the fifth one over from one of the taxiways. I was going through the count, and then I realised that my target wasn't there. It looked like someone had taken a spatula and scooped it off.'

Stimpert nevertheless dropped his bomb on the target coordinates that he had previously been given and then returned to base. When all the F-117 pilots were back in the debriefing room, Capt Neil McCaskill (Bandit No 299) looked at his tapes and said that he did not think his bomb had penetrated the HAS. After viewing it, the pilots looked at Stimpert's tape, which showed that McCaskill's target had clearly gone by the time the former had arrived for the second attack on the airfield. Both pilots immediately realised what had happened.

The big secondary explosion which Stimpert had seen in the distance had been set off by McCaskill's first bomb. The shelter had probably been a storage facility for fuel or weapons, and the GBU-27 had penetrated the roof and then exploded. Capt Stimpert said;

'On the original H-2 attack, all went well unless you were the guy attacking the second airfield. I'll always remember that night. As we were attacking, I realised that our targets were at the far end of the complex. Believe me, all the gunners on the ground were wide awake by then. The AAA was intense. I was flying about 30 degrees to the runway, trying to find my target with the sky lit up all around me from the rounds being fired at us.

'Off to my left was another F-117 flown by Capt Mike Mahon (Bandit No 293), and I could actually see his aircraft. That was very unnerving in the dark, but I was slightly above his release altitude. I was looking down on him, and I could clearly see his jet because the exhaust portion of his Nighthawk was glowing red. All four pilots in my strike package had their birds fire-walled, so were going as fast as we could.

'Off to the left, I could see a 57 mm gun firing away, with several people manning it. I then focused on dropping my bomb and timing it down. Impact came dead centre on the HAS. A split-second later, the entire IR display went into overload because there was a sizeable secondary explosion from my target. The fireball that emerged from it engulfed the gun emplacement that was firing in our direction.

'This was one of the first times we'd dropped bombs in what we called the vertical mode. This allowed the bomb to hit the target at a much less severe impact angle. It worked to perfection, and the concern about the weapon not penetrating the HAS from such a shallow angle immediately evaporated.'

The volume of AAA being fired into the sky over Baghdad reduced somewhat the longer the war went on, possibly because ammunition was running low or gun barrels were becoming worn out. A number of AAA sites had also been destroyed by day fighter-bombers. But those first nights over the city were highly dangerous, as every stealth pilot who flew these missions agrees. Capt John Hesterman participated in the first night strikes, and he continued on operations until the conflict came to an end. Here, he recalls his second mission, when he found himself below cloud cover – a situation which could have spelled disaster;

'The weather over Baghdad was bad those first few nights. On this mission I was trying to get below some low cloud so I could take out my target. As I was getting close to my run, I ran into a stream of AAA, which lasted for the entire length of my target run. I thought they knew I was coming, and checked to make sure I had thrown all the correct switches to render my jet stealthy. It turns out that the F-117 pilot in front of me had missed a turn and was running a little late – timing was easily thrown by weather – so what I was really looking at was the anti-aircraft fire trailing his flight path. Unfortunately it was the same as mine.

'I wanted to climb, but the fire appeared to be crossing overhead, and I wasn't wild about flying through it. The blast from one shell knocked both generators off line at one point and rolled the Nighthawk past 90 degrees. That was the only time I thought I was in real trouble – upside down in the dark, below my designated altitude and below clouds. One generator came back up quickly though, and the guys ahead got me back to the tanker and home because the INS never recovered. When I got close enough to King Khalid, I radioed in that I might have battle damage, but upon inspection after I landed my Nighthawk proved to be unmarked. It was a very lucky night for me.'

US strike aircraft dropped a total of 7400 tons of precision-guided (smart) bombs on assigned targets during _Desert Storm_, and no less than 90 per cent of this total was delivered by the F-117. The jet's primary weapon was the GBU-27, a live example of which is seen here with armourers from the 37th TFW(P) (_Air Force Association_)

'NUCLEAR' EXPLOSIONS

On several missions F-117 pilots saw spectacular explosions in the distance, with some being so impressive that they resembled a nuclear mushroom cloud. There were, of course, no nuclear explosions during the war, but some targets when hit generated massive secondary detonations.

By late January 1991 the key targets in Baghdad had been eliminated and the F-117s were hunting ammunition dumps, chemical storage facilities and bunkers elsewhere in the country. Lt Col Barry E Horne

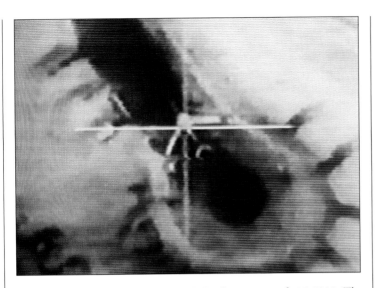

Early on in the war, Intelligence sources determined that the IrAF had armed Tu-16 bombers with chemical weapons, and was planning an imminent attack. F-117s were sent to counter this threat, and this photograph shows a Tu-16 square in the sights of a Nighthawk, which is about to release a GBU-10 *(USAF)*

recalled one of these missions, which he flew in aircraft 85-0818 *The Overachiever*;

'It was a two-target mission, and a confirmed ammunition bunker was my objective with my first bomb. The second one was destined for a chemical bunker. The ammunition dump was in central Iraq, 100 miles west of Baghdad. The second was just north of the Iraqi capital. I was flying at what we considered to be medium altitude, my jet being armed with GBU-27s. The ammunition dump was in a vast array of uniformly-placed bunkers in a flat, open area. Several had already been hit, but others remained intact. It was actually a double bunker configuration.

'I approached from south to north, and used only one weapon. Right after release, I detected that the thumb tracker was overly sensitive. That caused me considerable difficulty late in the delivery. At one point, the tracker caused the sight-line to move, or rather jump, approximately 100 ft south of the target. I regained control and managed to steer the weapon to final impact. The bomb hit precisely in the middle of the double bunker, striking the wall that separated them. The explosion was

In their protective shelters, the F-117s were parked one behind the other. When they emerged, the one in front was towed out and the other taxied out under its own power. These aircraft required a lot of attention during the day, as some of them were flying two missions a night *(Rose Reynolds)*

417th TFTS instructor Capt Kenneth Huff flew 12 combat missions between 1 February and war's end *(Ken Huff)*

absolutely brilliant. It seemed to engulf the sky all around me. For a moment I was afraid that it might even reach up and grab me.'

Lt Col Horne continued to his second target, where he scored another direct hit. He encountered no further problems with his tracker. At that point he left the area and headed back to the border. Looking to the west, he saw a bright orange glow coming from the direction of his first target – 20 minutes after the initial explosion, the fire had hardly subsided.

When Horne returned to base, Intelligence personnel and wing munitions experts viewed his tapes and stated that it was the largest explosion they had ever seen. It was estimated that the double bunker had contained more than a million pounds of explosives. Several F-117 pilots working in that area later reported seeing the fireworks, and being mystified about the cause. As Horne flew no further sorties in that area, he did not get to see the crater he assumed his attack had created.

417th TFTS

Pre-war, it had been decided by the 37th TFW that the 417th TFTS's role in *Desert Storm* was to provide replacement pilots and aircraft to make good any combat losses during the campaign's initial stages. When this proved unnecessary, pilots from the unit were rotated between the 415th and 416th TFSs.

Upon their arrival in-theatre, new pilots from Tonopah were required to fly single night and day practice missions over the Saudi ranges. They were also briefed on such topics as diversionary bases, refuelling procedures and escape and evasion tactics. Instructor Capt Kenneth Huff (Bandit No 275) was one of the 417th TFTS instructors who got to fly combat missions. Although his first did not come until 1 February, he was able to log 12 combat sorties before the air offensive ended. Here, Huff recalls that first mission, which he flew in aircraft 85-0814 *FINAL VERDICT*;

'The flight briefing always started with weather and Intel information, followed by an overall view of the game plan and then straight into the specifics. This would generally last 45-60 minutes, and we would then split up with our lead or wingman to cover any details not included in the main brief, such as tanker ops, who would jump off the tanker first and how much time there would be between our jump off times and the rendezvous after the strike.

'One thing that struck me that evening was when our squadron CO, Lt Col Bob Maher, came up and impressed upon me that I didn't have to deliver my bombs that night if the target weather was questionable. He told me it wasn't until his third mission over North Vietnam that he was able to drop his bombs, and that I shouldn't press my luck.

'I remember being very nervous about that first sortie, but when I got the engines started it was just like any other I'd flown over the ranges. My targets that night were two bridges – one spanning the Tigris River and the other over the Euphrates at Samawah and An Nasiriyah. My load comprised a pair of GBU-10s.

'As I got close to my first target, I was watching off to my right. It was fascinating to see all the AAA flying up from a distance down the river – I was making a mental note of their calibre. Since nothing was coming close to me, I thought this was going to be a cakewalk. When I set up on my target run, all systems were working fine and my timing was perfect. I threw my cursor out to the target and, sure enough, it was on a bridge. It seemed it was going to be easier than some of the training missions we had flown.

'I was aiming at the centre of three bridges in the IRADS (Infrared Acquisition and Designation System) sensor display, but the photo pack for my first target showed only a single bridge – now what? In the resulting confusion, I took a little longer than I should have locking onto the target. I quickly checked the contents of the second target photo pack and found a shot of the three bridges now directly in front of me – Intel had mixed up the order of my photos!

'Having hastily figured this out, I still managed to drop the target bridge with a GBU-10. As soon as the bomb hit, all hell broke loose, with AAA being fired in all directions. Fortunately, it was what we referred to as "bomb-activated AAA", so by the time it came up I was nearly out of range and moving away as fast as I could. The second bridge was easy to locate once I had the correct photos to compare with my display. My second bomb hit dead centre and, just like the first one, the ground fire then lit up. I'd finished my first sortie with two bridge kills. This was by far my most memorable mission.'

None of the pilots interviewed for this book talked about the specific altitudes they were flying at during their missions, as this remains classified information. They always referred to altitude in terms of high, medium or low, although low was only mentioned to describe target acquisition during bad weather.

Reflecting on an attack on the headquarters of Iraq's ruling Ba'ath Party in Baghdad, Capt Huff explained why they were locked into a specific altitude prior to taking off, with very little discretion to change it once in flight;

'This mission was flown during the final hours of the air war. When we were briefed for it, Col Whitley told us that the weather was going to be bad, and that we could go as low as necessary to acquire the target. This directive came from higher up, and the colonel was only passing on what had been relayed to him. We were told in the mass brief that once in the target area, we couldn't change altitudes until after we had dropped our

Weapons specialists prepare to attach the bomb guidance units which represented the key factor in the remarkable accuracy demonstrated by the F-117 pilots. Collateral damage and civilian casualties were kept to an absolute minimum even when targets were located in densely populated areas in Baghdad *(Rose Reynolds)*

ordnance because fellow pilots would be coming in from other directions at varying altitudes. We didn't want any mid-air collisions, so we were trapped down low.

'We were briefed to expect a 97 to 98 per cent moon, with overcast over Baghdad. Going into the target area, I couldn't make out anything with my IRADS, but I could see parts of the ground. I kept trying lower altitudes on the approach in an effort to acquire the target visually, but there was nothing. I finally dropped down very low to see if I could spot it – still nothing. Here I am, below overcast in a black aeroplane, with a nice bright white background highlighting me. That's when I noticed a AAA piece at my "one o'clock", firing right at me.

'Since I was on my target run, and the range to the gun emplacement was fairly short, my line of sight rate was too much for him. The tracers kept following me for what seemed like an eternity, but the gunners never pulled enough lead, as I kept seeing the orange dots curving behind me. Having flown as fast as I could, I succeeded in exiting the area and getting out of range.'

An unidentified Nighthawk pilot poses with the crew chief of F-117A 85-0814 *FINAL VERDICT*, which had logged 34 combat missions by war's end *(Wes Cockman)*

END GAME

By the time the 37th TFW(P) flew its last mission in *Desert Storm*, a typical F-117 pilot had logged between 100 and 150 hours of combat time over 43 nights of flying. Average sortie duration was between five-and-a-half and eight hours, depending on target location. It took around two-and-a-half hours just to reach the Iraqi border from King Khalid RSAFB in southwest Saudi Arabia.

Pilots were warned never to penetrate Iraqi airspace except during total darkness, and missions deep inside enemy territory were planned to ensure that returning aircraft would be crossing into friendly airspace by first light. Things did not always go as planned, but the airborne threat to the F-117s receded after the first few days of the air offensive.

A blue-banded inert 2000-lb GBU-27 training round is positioned for loading into the bomb-bay of this F-117 during pre-war training at King Khalid. The aircraft could carry two of these precision bombs, which it delivered with uncanny accuracy. This particular stealth aircraft was assigned to Capt T J 'Axel' Foley (Bandit No 327) *(Denny Lombard/Lockheed Martin)*

Other meteorological factors also had to be taken into account when mission planning, as Capt Rob Donaldson explained;

'We tried to make our attacks from west to east to take advantage of the jetstream in that area. I can remember one night when I was heading back from enemy territory. I was riding in a jetstream moving at about 200 knots. This didn't mean we were locked into this direction, because if we had, it could have helped the Iraqis figure things out. The direction of our attacks was changed quite often. Our F-117s

Capt Rob Donaldson poses proudly with members of his groundcrew just before taking off on another combat mission. This photograph was taken after dark inside one of the HASs at King Khalid (Rose Reynolds)

were subsonic, so we were always flying at full throttle when they were shooting in our direction.'

Just before the Coalition ground forces entered Iraq and Kuwait on 24 February 1991, the F-117 pilots were tasked with taking out selected targets in Kuwait City. Capt Michael Riehl flew on one of these missions, recalling;

'Only one target was assigned to me instead of the customary two, and that was the AT&T office building. Riyadh wanted it hit so that the Iraqis couldn't use the telephone exchange after the ground forces began their attacks. I was restricted to one run-in heading because there were mosques in the area which we'd been ordered to avoid at all cost.

'The mission was uneventful up until I dropped the weapon, which got thrown off a bit. As I went over the target, those big towers you see in all the pictures of Kuwait City rose up to block the laser beam in the final seconds of the bomb's delivery. Luckily, the LGB continued and hit the AT&T office, instead of following the laser's track onto the towers. It was just one of many breaks I got on some of my bomb drops.'

While the Saudi authorities were cooperative during the war – possibly because they feared that left unchecked, Saddam Hussein might have attempted an invasion – other countries were not expected to be quite as helpful. Several missions required the F-117 to fly close to the Syrian border, Capt Jeffrey Moore piloting aircraft 85-0834 *NECROMANCER* on one such sortie. His experiences during the course of the flight tend to confirm Syria's ambivalent attitude;

'One night, coming off the tanker en route to the stealth line where we cleaned the aeroplane up and put on the "Klingon Cloaking device", I was rocked by three concussions in close succession underneath my aircraft. After confirming all systems were in good order, I sucked up all the antennas, killed the lights and re-checked my position. I feared that a navigational error by the tanker or by me might have put me unexpectedly over bad guy country, but everything confirmed my position on the friendly side of the stealth line. Despite my RCS (radar cross-section) being an unknown due to possible blast damage, and the fear that maybe there was some skin damage to the aircraft, I decided to press on to the target.

'The mission went fine, and on my return to base I reported my experience to our Intelligence people, confirming my location at the time. My aircraft showed no damage. The next day, Intel unofficially confirmed my position as over ground held by our Syrian "allies". They pushed the report up to higher levels but nothing further happened, probably for political reasons. I'm convinced that the Syrians shot at me. There were several F-15 Eagles in the area at the time, and they confirmed the blast sightings.

'We avoided flying over or close to the Syrian border for the remainder of the war, although some routes from Kuwait and western target sites had to go across it due to geography and a need for fuel.'

THE WEATHER WORSENS

Paradoxically, the tempo of F-117 operations quickened as the air war began to wind down. Pilots and MPC personnel had already been pushed almost to their physical and mental limits, but still there was no let-up in the mission tasking from CENTAF – even though the end of operations was now in sight. Maj Shrader explained the effect that this seemingly endless cycle of missions had on the F-117 pilots, who still had a multitude of targets to destroy in ever-worsening weather;

'For us stealth guys, I believe the most dangerous part of the war was towards the end, when the number of sorties we were flying increased. We'd been phenomenally successful, and to my mind we were increasing the odds of someone catching the "Golden BB" (lucky AAA round). We were heavily tasked in and around Baghdad, and the weather was getting worse. This forced us to bring altitudes down to ensure that we had a good view of our targets so that we could destroy them.

'We offset the increased threat associated with attacking from lower altitudes by pulling off well coordinated multiple aircraft strikes. We could put a number of aircraft over some targets within a second or two and be gone before the first bomb impacted. This enabled us to destroy the enemy's remaining assets with the most destructive power, and it also meant that our aircraft weren't scattered all over the area for a prolonged

The state-of-the-art HASs at King Khalid could each accommodate two F-117s parked nose to tail, enabling maintenance and ordnance work to be done inside without exposure to the elements *(Ken Huff)*

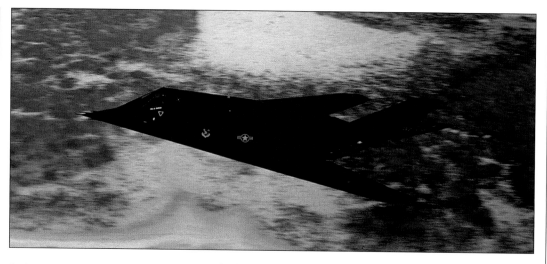

Bad weather conditions represented an almost-daily obstacle to air operations against Iraq by the F-117s. Many returned to King Khalid with their bombs because they could not get a clear view of their assigned targets. Some remote areas in northern Iraq near Mosul and Kirkuk were also blanketed in snow throughout the war *(37th TFW)*

period. This tactic worked to perfection, although if we had been early or late over a target, things could have been very bad for any one of us.

'If you were early, you would have destroyed the target solution for any aircraft behind you, as the bomb impact and explosion would prevent it from getting a good FLIR/DLIR lock. Effectively, you would have ruined the pilot's laser solution and blocked the view of his target. If you were late, your aircraft would invariably be the one that sucked up all the AAA rounds. To make matters worse, your view of the target would have also been blocked for the same reasons as previously described.

Maj Rod Shrader, a veteran of stealth operations in *Desert Storm*, prepares to climb out of the cockpit of his jet after a long flight from Nevada to Naval Air Station Memphis, in Tennessee. This photograph was taken in October 1991, when the F-117 was the biggest attraction at US airshows *(Author)*

Immediately after the war had ended, US forces inspecting the IrAF's heavily damaged air base at Tallil found this poorly-copied document, which had probably come from a western magazine, posted on the operations board. It was intended to help those MiG fighter pilots trained to fly at night to recognise the F-117's distinctive silhouette, should they have come into close contact with one. Note that the B-2 silhouette was also featured on the document *(Luke Atwell)*

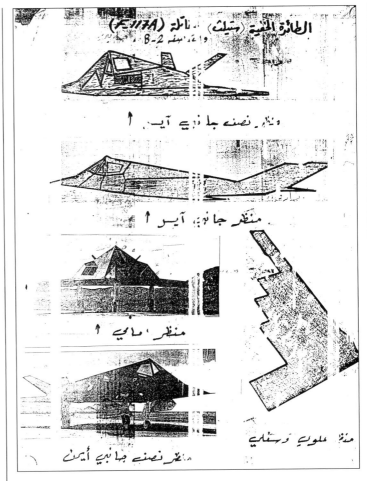

'If all bombs were dropped within a few seconds of each other, then the pilot had a good view to lock-on. He also had time to exit the area before impact. This reinforced principles we had held for years. In the stealth world, you have to be able to strike your target within a second of when you are supposed to. If you can't, then you remove the one thing that makes our capabilities so extraordinary. The rule we lived by was that if you were early or late on a multi-ship mission, don't drop your bomb – go on to your second target.'

The world's media reported that the air war was now beginning to wind down as February drew to a close, but there was still no way of knowing how long the ground war would last. The pace escalated considerably during that period, and according to Maj Rod Shrader, the tempo increased to about 64 sorties per night. This meant that nearly two-dozen F-117s were flying two missions in one night.

This USAF chart shows the number of F-117s that participated in *Desert Storm* by date of commitment. As can be seen, the *Desert Shield* build-up took several months to complete *(Rob Donaldson)*

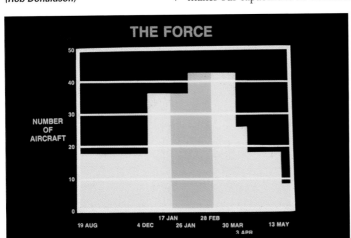

The 37th TFW(P) committed a total of 42 Nighthawks to the air offensive. This encompassed two full squadrons (415th and 416th TFS), plus six aircraft from the 417th TFTS. The maintenance folks worked hard to keep them flying, as did the ordnance loaders and the MPC personnel. Running the schedule required a 24-hour-a-day effort from most of those involved. Maj Shrader, who usually flew aircraft 88-0841 *Mystic Warrior*, explained the cost of maintaining such a punishing schedule;

'I think it was fortunate that the war stopped when it did. Our aircrews were at the point of exhaustion, especially those who had to go straight from a mission to the MPC. There just wasn't time to get rested up before you had to go again. During this brief period, I don't know how we got through without a scratch. We were flying in very bad weather, which forced us lower, yet still we came through in good shape.'

Maj Shrader flew *Mystic Warrior* of the 416th TFS on most of the 18 combat missions that it tallied in *Desert Storm*. This aircraft was not popular amongst pilots of the 37th TFW(P), which may explain why it completed so few sorties – most of the 42 F-117s in-theatre averaged around 35 missions each. An explanation as to why *Mystic Warrior* was shunned by most is provided by Maj Shrader;

'It had the world's most sensitive tracker (finger button), but once you got used to it, the target could easily be pinpointed. You always knew which way the tracker was going to drift, and how to adjust your finger to make sure that you followed the target okay. I flew it on the first night of the war and was very successful against two targets. The aeroplane remained fully serviceable throughout the entire campaign.'

It was just before *Desert Storm* ended that the tempo of F-117 missions reached its highest level, and that in turn increased the risk of mistakes being made. Capt David Francis recalled one frustrating mission near war's end when Capt Mike Riehl was flying as his wingman;

'As our squadron was ordered to send out more and more aircraft each night, the opportunity for missing little items during planning increased. We took off and headed for our tanker rendezvous point. When we

Some 37th TFW(P) F-117 missions lasted nearly eight hours, and even the shorter ones took more than five. After 43 nights of combat, most of the pilots involved had accumulated well over 100 hours in the cockpit *(Rose Reynolds)*

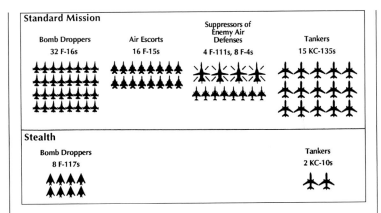

Standard Mission			
Bomb Droppers 32 F-16s	Air Escorts 16 F-15s	Suppressors of Enemy Air Defenses 4 F-111s, 8 F-4s	Tankers 15 KC-135s

Stealth	
Bomb Droppers 8 F-117s	Tankers 2 KC-10s

This USAF briefing diagram demonstrates the F-117's value in *Desert Storm*. It would take all the conventional aircraft in a standard mission strike package to destroy such high value enemy assets as nuclear facilities or major airfields, but just eight Nighthawks, supported by two KC-10s, could accomplish the same task *(USAF)*

reached it, there was no tanker in the area. I broke radio silence to see if there were any on our frequency and got no answer. We discovered that the hook-up time we'd been given was 30 minutes later than that given to the tanker crew. If we'd waited that long we'd have missed our TOT, so I looked at the map and picked some coordinates at our point of no return. We wouldn't have had enough fuel to return to King Khalid. I radioed the tanker, gave them the coordinates and asked if they could be there in 20 minutes. The answer was that they'd try. We reached the area and there was still no tanker in sight.

'Just as we were going to turn and head back to base, the tanker turned on its lights just like a big Christmas tree. We were able to top off quickly and proceed north. We made our TOT, but ran into another glitch – the weather was so bad we were unable to drop our bombs. But because the tanker crew had proved so flexible, at least we had the opportunity to try.'

Being a radarless aircraft, the Nighthawk depended on its infrared and laser capabilities. Targeting calculations had to be made using accurate

Groundcrew tow in Maj Wesley Wyrick's F-117, which has just completed its mission for the night. During the war's first night, the Nighthawks attacked 31 per cent of the targets bombed in Iraq, despite representing just 2.5 per cent of the total Coalition inventory *(Denny Lombard/Lockheed Martin)*

satellite photography prior to the aircraft being sortied. Once in the air, pilots had to place their FLIR/DLIR cross-hairs on a pre-set point, such as a highway intersection or soccer pitch, en route to the target. When pilots began their final approach, they would laser the landmarks and the system would automatically update itself. When the bomb was dropped it was usually a direct hit. In fact, few senior commanders realised that this precision had become a significant force multiplier. It was hard to convince them that when the Nighthawk was assigned to attack a particular target, that target was as good as destroyed, and that one pass was usually enough.

Maj Wesley Wyrick explained how, on several missions to the same area, he used an SA-2 site to update his system. However, several days into the war the site had been taken out – once top-priority targets such as SAM sites were destroyed, the stealth pilots started attacking secondary ones. Maj Wyrick said;

'This led to what we called "theme nights". At that time the Iraqis were firing a lot of Scud missiles at Israel. They wanted us to try and find the launchers, so we went Scud hunting for a few nights. We were actually performing an armed reconnaissance mission. If one of our guys stumbled onto one, they were authorised to kill it. These were called "Scud nights". Then we had "SAM nights", when our guys made thorough sweeps north and south of Baghdad. We took out quite a few of them. This enabled our B-52s to get in closer.

'During the final few days of the air war, and right before the ground war began, we did "Fire Trench night", hitting every one of those north of Kuwait City. The Iraqis had dug a series of trenches, and under each one was a network of oil pipes that fed directly into the trench. We could see the oil pipes with our infrared – they were like a big sprinkler system fed by diverter heads every few miles to control the flow of oil to the areas that were to burn, thus preventing our ground forces from advancing. We popped all the heads and it released oil into the trenches. An hour after we hit them Marine Corps fast jets came in with napalm and burned up all the oil.

'By the time our troops began to move, there was no oil in the system to burn, and no way for the Iraqis to pump more into the network. But when

During the first nights of the *Desert Storm* air campaign, F-117s were the only aircraft attacking targets in downtown Baghdad. They took out all the most critical targets, paving the way for attacks by other types. Here, Capt John Peterson (Bandit No 347) poses alongside GBU-27 LGBs which have been loaded onto the trapezes fitted into the bomb-bay of Capt Savidge's *FINAL VERDICT (Wes Cockman)*

Saddam Hussein set fire to the oil wells in Kuwait, and we were flying in that area, we had to try and attack our targets by approaching from beneath the smoke. It was absolutely amazing how much smoke and haze there was.'

Another pilot flying on a fire trench mission was Capt John Savidge (Bandit No 322). On 15 February he was flying one night and mission planning the next, whilst trying to find time for much-needed sleep in between. It was not an easy task, as he recalled;

'The commanding general of the Marine Corps' ground forces decided that those trenches could become a liability when they got orders to cross them. He presented his problem to high command at Riyadh and asked for their help. Our liaison people said we could do the job.

'The trenches were huge and covered a vast area. They'd been dug while we were building up our forces in *Desert Shield*. Our targets were not the trenches themselves, but the pumping stations spaced out over their

Pictured second from left is Capt John Savidge, whose airline flight attendant fiancée sent him the appropriately-dressed 'Barbie' doll which has been taped to the 2000-lb GBU-10 behind the men. A message scrawled on the bomb read 'Barbie Does Baghdad' *(John Savidge)*

The air campaign ended for the F-117 pilots on 28 February 1991, when the third wave of jets, which was to have been launched in the early hours of that morning, was cancelled at the last minute following orders received from HQ. This brought 43 gruelling nights of dangerous missions to a close *(Rose Reynolds)*

Maj Bob Eskridge (Bandit No 278) is pictured with Capt John Savidge's *FINAL VERDICT* during the war's final days. The jet is loaded with two GBU-27s and displays 30+ mission symbols under its canopy rail *(Wes Cockman)*

entire length. The pipes from these pumps were at least six feet in diameter.

'I helped plan and brief the missions, and they were carried out to perfection. There was one small glitch, however – the weather was so bad over the area that everything was delayed for one night. A short time later we heard through channels that the Marine Corps commander was very pleased with what we'd done.'

Prior to *Desert Storm*, it was well known that the Iraqi air defence system was the most technologically advanced and sophisticated that American air power could possibly face. Indeed, Iraq's long war with Iran had barely dented its military capacity. The F-117, and its associated technology, had become available just at the right time. Saddam Hussein and his senior commanders could not have been aware of its capability before the first nights of the Coalition air offensive.

Even though the war had ended, F-117 pilots remained on alert in case the Iraqis refused to honour the strict conditions of their surrender. These pilots belong to the 416th TFS, and their CO, Lt Col Greg Gonyea, is standing second from right *(Rod Shrader)*

As the air war neared its end, these F-117 pilots took the chance to unwind. On the ground is Maj Bob Eskridge, kneeling on him is Capt John Peterson and at far right is Capt Matthew Byrd (Bandit No 348) *(Ken Huff)*

VIPs visit King Khalid as the war draws to a close. They are, from left to right, 37th TFW(P) CO Col Alton Whitley, Congressman Sam Nunn (Georgia), Lt Gen Charles A Horner, Congressman John Warner (Virginia) and unidentified. The visit was prompted by the success achieved by the F-117s and their pilots *(Rose Reynolds)*

Col Alton C Whitley Jr (second from right) discusses a problem with one of his maintenance crew and several of his pilots at King Khalid during the latter stages of the air offensive *(Wes Cockman)*

The real key to success, however, was the professionalism of the personnel involved in the aircraft's operation. It was the discipline and skill of the F-117 pilots which enabled the Nighthawks to destroy more than half of all the high priority targets scattered over Iraq, and all of those within the city of Baghdad. This feat was accomplished with just 42 jets – a tiny proportion of the total number of Coalition combat aircraft committed to the air offensive.

Lt Col Bob Maher neatly summed up the effectiveness of Nighthawk missions over Iraq when he stated;

'During my brief stint in *Desert Storm*, I was assigned many targets ranging from isolated communications antennas through to aircraft shelters, railway yards, weapons storage bunkers and Baghdad's nuclear research facility. I think that just about every one of my fellow F-117 pilots also covered this list of targets with outstanding results. The Nighthawk operated in combat just as it did in the deserts of Nevada – a wonderfully accurate platform and, more importantly, one which brought its pilot home 100 per cent of the time.'

Another factor behind the jet's success was leadership. Many of the pilots who flew with the 37th TFW(P) praised Col Al Whitley as a great leader, and one who was perfect for the job in hand. They said that he had allowed his tacticians to plan the missions, and had then permitted his pilots to execute them without interference. Whitley had great confidence in his people. When a problem cropped up he fought for them, and usually won.

It was this management philosophy which had allowed the F-117 and its pilots to demonstrate to the world what this unique weapons system was capable of achieving in combat. And the statistics leave no doubt as to what that was.

The war has ended, and a group of weary pilots stretch their legs after the long flight back from Saudi Arabia to Langley AFB. They would overnight in Virginia, before returning to Tonopah the next day *(Wes Cockman)*

APPENDICES

APPENDIX I

F-117 COMBAT CHRONOLOGY OF MISSIONS IN THE FIRST AND LAST TEN DAYS OF OPERATION *DESERT STORM*

The first missions were flown on the night of 17 January 1991 and the last on 27 February. The first few waves of F-117s from the 37th TFW(P), which attacked targets in Iraq, were tasked with the destruction of Saddam Hussein's command and control centres. Their success determined the ability of the day fighter-bombers to penetrate Iraqi airspace in relative safety.

17 January
Day One, first wave
At 0022 hrs, the first wave of F-117s is launched against targets at Nukhayb, Baghdad, Al Taqaddum and several other locations, most of which lie between the Iraqi border and Baghdad. Their destruction opens a corridor for other aircraft. Also included on the target list is the IrAF HQ, plus radar and telephone facilities. The strike force comprises ten 415th TFS F-117s. Despite bad weather, the bombs that are dropped score well against intended targets.

Day One, second wave
A second wave, comprising 12 F-117s, is launched against many targets in and around Baghdad, a number of which have already been hit by the first wave. New targets include the presidential bunker in Baghdad, the airfield at Al-Rasheed, radio and television transmitters.

Day One, third wave
The night's final attack comprises eight F-117s, which attack targets on the priority list. This includes ammunition dumps and various HQ buildings. All aircraft return unscathed, as do those in the first two waves.

18 January
Day Two, first wave
Pressure to eliminate command and control targets continues. The 415th TFS launches 12 aircraft, with one abort, to strike targets in the Baghdad area. They include radio transmitters, command and control bunkers and the Iraqi national computer centre.

Day Two, second wave
The 416th TFS shoulders most of the target burden with 12 aircraft. Some targets lie outside greater Baghdad, and the list includes fresh ones such as a major nuclear reactor and ammunition bunkers. Again, some of the F-117s are tasked with finishing off command and control centres within the city.

19 January
Day Three, first wave
The 415th TFS sends ten F-117s to attack the Iraqi Ministry of Defence and IrAF HQ complex. Target area weather is even worse than the night before.

Day Three, second wave
Most key command and control centres are now believed to have been eliminated, but a few F-117s from this wave are sent in to make sure. Also included are Scud missile sites. Bad weather forces many pilots to attack alternate targets.

20 January
Day Four, first wave
Weather still a major factor. The 415th TFS launches a number of aircraft against command and control bunkers, operations centres, ammunition storage facilities, telephone exchanges and radio transmitter stations not just in Baghdad, but scattered over a wide area.

Day Four, second wave
The weather improves, leading to more bombs being dropped. This wave involves nine 416th TFS F-117s attacking similar targets to the first wave and the previous night. Ammunition storage dumps continue to be on the mission list. Chemical and biological warfare centres are also given high priority.

21 January
Day Five, first wave
Ten 415th TFS aircraft are assigned to attack biological warfare facilities, a television transmitter/radio relay terminal and, again, the IrAF HQ. The IrAF has by now been decimated, with its remaining assets hidden in hardened and camouflaged shelters which will be methodically destroyed by 'bunker-busting' GBU-27 bombs.

Day Five, second wave
The 416th TFS again flies most missions on this wave, which concentrates on ammunition dumps and Scud missile bunkers. Some SAM sites are also targeted.

22 January
Day Six, first wave
The 415th TFS sends 14 F-117s to attack communications transmitters, telephone exchanges and a nuclear research centre in Baghdad. Weather is good and 20 direct hits are scored on designated targets, as most aircraft are able to drop at least one bomb.

Day Six, second wave
The 416th TFS launches 14 aircraft to concentrate on Baghdad targets, including the IrAF's HQ, SAM sites and the Ministry of Defence building. Clear weather helps make this the most productive wave of the war to date, with 26 direct hits. Command and control centres are 90 per cent destroyed, depriving Iraqi ground forces of information from other areas.

23 January
Day Seven, first wave
With 14 415th TFS aircraft attacking Balad South-East airfield at specific intervals, this is the first time a major concentration of F-117s has been sent to strike one target, and 21 hits are recorded. Many of the HASs dispersed over a wide area are full of enemy fighters.

Day Seven, second wave
Ten 416th TFS stealth aircraft strike a wide variety of targets, including some within Baghdad and several further down the priority list such as bridges over the River Euphrates. The weather is good and numerous direct hits are confirmed.

24 January
Day Eight, first wave
One of the worst nights for weather, and from the 12+ 415th TFS aircraft that are despatched only three bombs are dropped because targets cannot be positively identified.

Day Eight, second wave

Fourteen 416th TFS F-117s attack a major airfield, communication centres and other bridges not destroyed by bombings during the day.

25 January
Day Nine, first wave

The tempo increases with a return to three-wave tasking, with the first flown by 13 aircraft from the 416th TFS, which attack major airfields at Al Assad, Qayyarah West and Kirkuk. The weather is good and some 20 bomb hits are scored.

Day Nine, second wave

The 416th TFS attacks road bridges.

Day Nine, third wave

Ten 415th and 416th TFS aircraft attack the airfield at Tallil, but bad weather over the target area prevents the mission from being successful.

26 January
Day Ten, first wave

Six F-117s from the two squadrons attack HASs at Tallil airfield and destroy several bridges.

Day Ten, second wave

The mission is split into two sections with four 415th TFS aircraft launched at 2200 hrs, and another four departing King Khalid one hour later. Their targets are H-2 and H-3 airfields in western Iraq. Improving weather means that the results achieved by aircraft in this wave are much better than those of the first wave.

FINAL TEN NIGHTS OF OPERATIONS

18 February
Day 33, first wave

The objective is nuclear research facilities in Baghdad, but bad weather causes the attack to be shifted to secondary targets.

Day 34, second wave

Fourteen aircraft from both squadrons attack hangars at Baghdad's Muthenna airfield and ammunition storage facilities, achieving 26 direct hits thanks to good weather.

Day 34, third wave

Small number of F-117s attack two airfields and a mountainside weapons cache which is sealed off by bomb hits.

19 February
Day 35, first wave

Target numbers dwindle and some repeat attacks are made to ensure success. Targets including Baghdad nuclear research facilities, a major ammunition storage area at Karbala and a solid propellant plant at Latifiya are hit by a total of no fewer than 28 bombs.

20 February
Day 35, second wave

Ten Nighthawks attack Jalibah South-East airfield and HASs, but bad weather prevents bombs being dropped.

Day 36, first wave

Aircraft from 415th and 416th TFSs attack key railway bridges and a chemical plant and 17 direct hits are scored, ensuring destruction of targets. The weather is variable, but pilots who drop their bombs have a good view of their targets.

21 February
Day 36, second wave

Another visit to Al Taqaddum airfield completes destruction of existing targets, based on satellite imagery. F-117s from both squadrons also attack a rocket plant, ammunition depots and an arms factory in one of the most productive waves flown, which sees 26 bombs score direct hits.

Day 37, first wave

Six 416th TFS F-117s and four from the 415th TFS attack several targets, scoring 17 solid hits on ammunition storage facilities and chemical production plants based on latest Intelligence data. Years later, further information will indicate the sheer number of such facilities in Iraq.

Day 37, second wave

Fourteen Nighthawks from both squadrons attack biological weapons production and storage facilities using up-to-date Intelligence reports. H-2 airfield is attacked again.

22 February
Day 37, third wave

Further attacks are made on priority targets to ensure destruction. This wave strikes ammunition storage bunkers, an underground nuclear plant and a factory known to produce Scud missiles.

Day 38, first wave

Four 415th TFS Nighthawks and six from the 416th TFS hit targets in and around Baghdad. Five strike a research facility and put all ten of their bombs on the target. A Scud missile production facility is also hit again.

Day 38, second wave

With the end of the war less than a week away, a major effort is launched against the nuclear research plant in Baghdad, with 14 F-117s scoring 19 direct hits.

23 February
Day 38, third wave

Ten Nighthawks attack Iraqi Intelligence and Special Operations HQ, with 15 LGBs placed dead centre on their targets.

Day 39, first wave

In a move to assist Coalition ground troops' initial thrusts into Iraq and Kuwait, the 37th TFW(P) despatches 31 Nighthawks in a single wave, each jet departing at one minute intervals, from King Khalid. Many targets are located within the city of Baghdad. Most major Iraqi assets have now been destroyed, but there are still many secondary targets remaining.

24 February
Day 39, second wave

Weather worsens after first wave attack, and the second wave of six F-117s has difficulty in dropping bombs. Some pilots return with their LGBs.

Day 40, first wave

Ten Nighthawks attack several lesser targets and record 19 direct hits.

Day 40, second wave

Fourteen F-117s attack an assortment of smaller factories, with the special security services building in Baghdad, ammunition bunkers and other targets now being given higher priority. Records show that aircraft video footage indicates 18 direct hits.

25 February
Day 40, third wave

Bad weather over Baghdad prevents bombs being dropped on their assigned targets. Others elsewhere in Iraq are attacked, and 11 hits are achieved.

Day 41, first, second and third wave

Bad weather encountered by the earlier wave prompts HQ to cancel the remainder of the night's missions. This weather pattern will continue into the next night.

26 February

Day 42, first wave

A maximum catch-up effort is ordered to make up for the previous day's scrubbed missions, and each squadron launches 16 aircraft. However, the weather remains bad, and as a result of the strict policy which states that no weapons can be dropped without a positive target lock, most aircraft return with their bombs.

27 February

Day 42, second wave

Results a little better, although still affected by weather, with 27 sorties flown but only eight bombs dropped. Some good hits are still achieved.

Day 43, first wave

The weather clears and both squadrons launch ten aircraft apiece, which record 32 direct hits. Most LGBs are dropped on Ba'ath Party HQ and Baghdad's Muthenna. Several other less important targets are also hit.

Day 43, second wave

The air campaign is rapidly winding down, but five F-117s from each squadron nevertheless hit a missile development and production plant and a rocket motor facility. HQ cancels the next wave before midnight and wing CO, Col Al Whitley, is ordered to put all future missions on hold. At 0015 hrs CENTAF halts operations, pending Iraq's signature of the cease-fire agreement.

28 February

Desert Calm

APPENDIX II

PILOTS PARTICIPATING IN OPERATION *DESERT STORM*

When a pilot checked out in the F-117 he was given a Bandit number, and they were allocated in numerical order

Jerry Leatherman, No 259	Jerry Sink, No 294	Mike Mahan, No 323
Greg Feest, No 261	Joseph Salata, No 295	Russell Travis, No 324
Jimmy Villers, No 262	Lee Gustin, No 297	Paul Dolson, No 325
Mark Renelt, No 264	Dan DeCamp, No 298	Terry Foley, No 327
Nick Santangelo, No 265	Neil McAskill, No 299	Steve Edgar, No 328
Jim Mastny, No 268	Al Minnich, No 300	Greg Gonyea, No 329
Don Backhus, No 269	Blake Bourland, No 301	Wesley Wyrick, No 330
Scott Stimpert, No 270	Dennis Baker, No 302	Joe Bouley, No 331
Frank Holmes, No 273	Brian Foley, No 303	Lou McDonald, No 332
Bobby Bledsoe, No 274	Chuck Link, No 305	Clare Whitescarver, No 333
Ken Huff, No 275	Phil McDaniel, No 306	Steve Troyer, No 334
Don Chapman, No 276	Mark Lindstrom, No 307	Kevin Tarrant, No 335
Bob Eskridge, No 278	Bob Maher, No 308	Rich Treadway, No 336
Steve Marquez, No 279	Gregg Verser, No 310	Ray Lynott, No 337
George Kelman, No 281	Miles Pound, No 311	Dale Zelko, No 338
Klaus Klause, No 283	Rod Shrader, No 312	John Hesterman, No 339
Marcel Kerdavid, No 284	Leo Broline, No 313	Steve Farnham, No 340
Jerry Carpenter, No 285	Barry Horne, No 314	Lee Archambault, No 341
Tim Phillips, No 286	Robert Saroski, No 315	Steve Chappel, No 342
Ralph Getchel, No 287	R C Cline, No 316	Mike Christensen, No 343
Kim Fieldstad, No 288	Dave Francis, No 317	Robert Huff, No 344
Jon Boyd, No 289	Wes Cockman, No 318	Bruce Kreidler, No 345
Lorin Long, No 290	Drew Nichols, No 319	Don Higgins, No 346
Bob Warren, No 291	Mike Riehl, No 320	John Peterson, No 347
Jeff Moore, No 292	Rob Donaldson, No 321	Matt Byrd, No 348
Mike Mahon, No 293	John Savidge, No 322	

APPENDIX III

Lessons of Stealth:
Application of the F-117A in the Gulf War

Iraqi Force Effectiveness

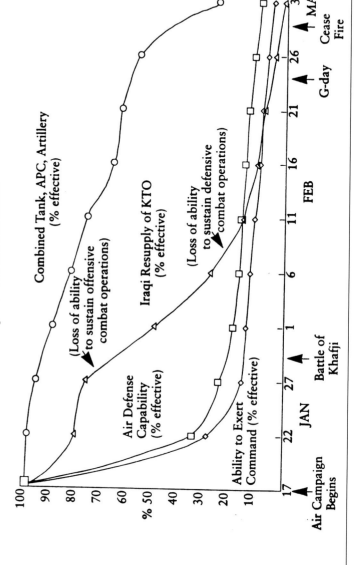

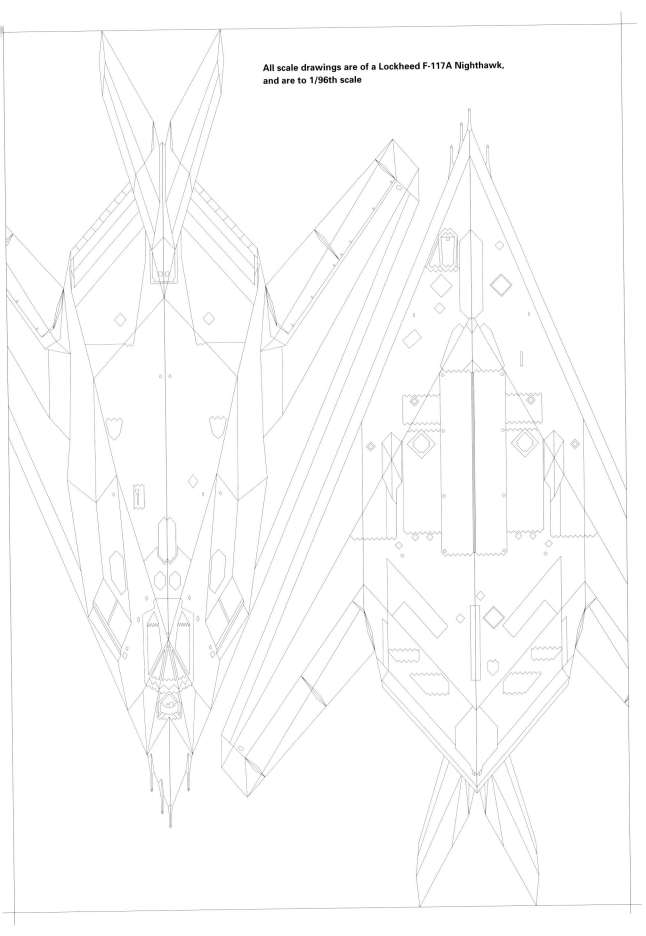

All scale drawings are of a Lockheed F-117A Nighthawk,
and are to 1/96th scale

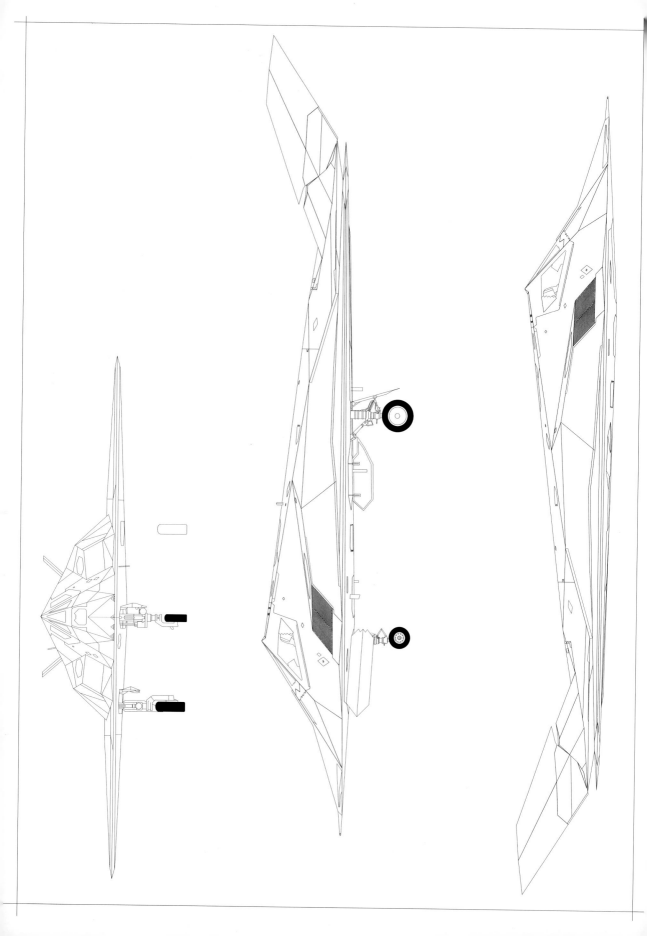

COLOUR PLATES

1
F-117A 81-10796 *FATAL ATTRACTION*, assigned to Capt Daniel DeCamp, 415th TFS/37th TFW(P), King Khalid RSAFB, January 1991
Only the 12th production-standard F-117A built, this aircraft was amongst the 22 jets initially deployed to Saudi Arabia on 26/27 August 1990 as part of Operation *Desert Shield*. A veteran of 29 combat missions during *Desert Storm*, it presently serves with the 49th FW's 9th FS at Holloman AFB, New Mexico.

2
F-117A 81-10798 *ACES AND EIGHTS*, assigned to Maj Joseph Bouley, 415th TFS/37th TFW(P), King Khalid RSAFB, February 1991
Another early-build F-117, this aircraft already boasted bomb-bay door art when it was assigned to Maj Bouley. This almost certainly means that the Nighthawk's nickname was bestowed upon it by the enlisted personnel that regularly serviced the jet. 81-10798 flew 34 combat missions in *Desert Storm*. Twelve years later, it was back in action over Iraq once again when 81-10798 was one of a dozen F-117s deployed to Al Udeid air base, in Qatar, by the 49th FW's 8th FS to serve with the 379th Air Expeditionary Wing. 81-10798 completed a further 13 missions in Operation *Iraqi Freedom*. The jet presently serves with the 49th FW's 9th FS.

3
F-117A 82-0803 *UNEXPECTED GUEST*, assigned to Capt Scott Stimpert, 416th TFS/37th TFW(P), King Khalid RSAFB, February 1991
The artwork and name displayed on the bomb-bay door of this aircraft were credited to the jet's crew chief, who took inspiration from the 1982 album of the same name by British heavy metal group Demon. By war's end, 33 mission symbols adorned 82-0803. This aircraft was one of eight Nighthawks to participate in Operation *Just Cause* on 19 December 1989, when US forces seized President Manuel Noriega in Panama. Almost a decade later, in March 1999, 82-0803 was one of 25 F-117s flown in combat by the 49th FW over Serbia and Kosovo as part of the USAF's commitment to Operation *Allied Force*. Amongst the ten Nighthawks deployed by the 8th FS to Aviano air base, in Italy, the aircraft flew 29 missions from both this location and Spangdahlem air base, in Germany. 82-0803 is still presently assigned to the 8th FS.

4
F-117A 83-0807 *THE CHICKENHAWK*, assigned to Maj Steve Edgar, 415th TFS/37th TFW(P), King Khalid RSAFB, January 1991
Another of the early arrivals at King Khalid in August 1990, this jet was named by its maintenance personnel before being assigned to Maj Edgar. The latter was flying 82-0807 when he participated in the strikes on the nuclear research centre on the outskirts of Baghdad on 18 January 1991. Edgar also used the aircraft to bomb Iraqi defensive oil trenches in the last few days of the war. Something of a 'hangar queen', *THE CHICKENHAWK* only managed 14 missions during *Desert Storm* – the second lowest tally (only 81-0797 flew fewer, completing just eight missions) for the 42 F-117s involved in the conflict. Like 82-0803, this aircraft also saw action in Operation *Allied Force* in 1999, being one of nine jets deployed by the 49th FW's 9th FS – it still serves with this unit today.

5
F-117A 84-0810 *DARK ANGEL*, assigned to Maj Jon Boyd, 416th TFS/37th TFW(P), King Khalid RSAFB, February 1991
Although assigned to Maj Boyd, this aircraft was also flown by several other pilots from both the 415th and 416th TFSs during *Desert Storm*. Maj Boyd's first mission in 84-0810 was a strike on the heavily defended intercept operations centre at H-3 airfield, in western Iraq. A veteran of 26 combat missions, 84-0810 also saw action in Operation *Allied Force* in 1999 with the 49th FW's 9th FS. The aircraft still presently serves with this unit.

6
F-117A 84-0812 *Axel*, assigned to Capt Brian Foley, 415th TFS/37th TFW(P), King Khalid RSAFB, February 1991
84-0812 has the distinction of flying the most combat missions by an F-117 in *Desert Storm*, the jet completing 42 in total. Its assigned pilot, Capt 'Axel' Foley, was also responsible for naming the aircraft. 84-0812 is presently assigned to the 49th FW's 7th FS.

7
F-117A 85-0813 *THE TOXIC AVENGER*, assigned to Col Alton Whitley, 37th TFW(P), King Khalid RSAFB, February 1991
Assigned to the CO of the 37th TFW(P), this aircraft was one of four jets at King Khalid to bear wing titling on its ruddervators. Appropriately, Col Whitley flew 85-0813 on the first night of the air war as part of the second wave of F-117s sent to attack targets in Baghdad. By the end of the conflict it had flown 35 combat missions. The jet's groundcrew, SSgt Gerald Bies and Sgts Donald Birkett and Ronald Harmon, were responsible for its name, which was also the title of a 1962 'B' movie. The artwork carried on the bomb-bay door was inspired by a 1976 album released by British heavy metal band Iron Maiden. Also a veteran of Operation *Just Cause*, 85-0813 is presently assigned to the 49th FW's 9th FS.

8
F-117A 85-0814 *FINAL VERDICT*, assigned to Capt Kenneth Huff, 416th TFS/37th TFW(P), King Khalid RSAFB, February 1991

Originally assigned to Capt John T Savidge, this aircraft was also flown by Capt Huff among others. With a total of 34 sorties over Iraq and Kuwait recorded, it won an award at war's end for being the best overall performer on combat missions. Amongst the missions flown by 85-0814 were successful attacks on major bridges over the rivers Tigris and Euphrates. Its crew chief throughout the campaign was Sgt Kiilani Keeter. This aircraft presently serves with the 49th FW's 9th FS.

9

F-117A 85-0816 *LONE WOLF*, assigned to Maj Gregory A Feest, 415th TFS/37th TFW(P), King Khalid RSAFB, January 1991

Maj Feest was flying this aircraft when he dropped the first bomb of *Desert Storm* in the early hours of 17 January 1991. He had performed a similar feat in the same aircraft during Operation *Just Cause* on 19 December 1989, when the F-117 made its combat debut over Panama. *LONE WOLF* was another of *Desert Storm's* top-performing Nighthawks, completing 39 combat missions.

10

F-117A 85-0818 *The Overachiever*, assigned to Lt Col Barry E Horne, 415th TFS/37th TFW(P), King Khalid RSAFB, January 1991

Devoid of two-letter wing codes on its ruddervators as carried by most F-117s at King Khalid, but boasting a bigger Tactical Air Command emblem, this aircraft finished the war with 38 mission symbols below its canopy rail. Lt Col Horne was flying 85-0818 when he dropped a bomb on a double bunker in an ammunition dump 100 west of Baghdad in north central Iraq. The bunker detonated with such force that from many miles away it looked like a small nuclear explosion. After viewing the video footage, ordnance specialists estimated that the installation had contained more than one million pounds of explosives. Yet another Operation *Just Cause* veteran, 85-0818 also saw action in Operation *Allied Force* in 1999 with the 49th FW's 8th FS. The aircraft still presently serves with this unit.

11

F-117A 86-0821 *SNEAK ATTACK*, assigned to Maj Wesley Wyrick, 415th TFS/37th TFW(P), King Khalid RSAFB, February 1991

Maj Wyrick was among the 415th TFS pilots to initially deploy to Saudi Arabia in late August 1990. His Nighthawk eventually flew a total of 32 combat missions, including hunts for Scud missiles and attacks on the Ba'ath Party HQ in Baghdad. 86-0821 was yet another *Desert Storm* veteran to see further action in Operation *Allied Force* in 1999, flying with the 49th FW's 9th FS. The aircraft is still presently flying with this unit.

12

F-117A 84-0825 *"MAD-MAX"*, assigned to Lt Col Ralph Getchell, 415th TFS/37th TFW(P), King Khalid RSAFB, February 1991

Assigned to the CO of the 415th TFS, this aircraft was one of four jets at King Khalid to bear wing titling on its ruddervators. Named by its crew chief, it too had deployed to Saudi Arabia in August 1990. Lt Col Getchell flew several different Nighthawks during his tour, and the 33 missions logged by 84-0825 during *Desert Storm* were flown by a handful of pilots. This aircraft is presently serving with the 49th FW's 8th FS.

13

F-117A 84-0826 *NACHTFALKE*, assigned to Capt Rob Donaldson, 415th TFS/37th TFW(P), King Khalid RSAFB, February 1991

Nachtfalke means nighthawk in German, and Capt Donaldson named his aircraft in honour of a close friend from Germany. The 'Donald Duck' artwork credited to the aircraft's crew chief was derived from the original Walt Disney drawing created in 1943 for the 415th Night Fighter Squadron when it was equipped with Bristol Beaufighters in the Mediterranean theatre. 84-0826 flew 34 combat missions during *Desert Storm*, and also saw action in Operation *Allied Force* in 1999, flying with the 49th FW's 9th FS. The aircraft is still presently assigned to this unit.

14

F-117A 85-0830 *BLACK ASSASSIN*, assigned to Maj Robert D Eskridge, 416th TFS/37th TFW(P), King Khalid RSAFB, February 1991

The appropriately named *BLACK ASSASSIN* was credited with completing 31 combat missions over Iraq during its *Desert Storm* stint. Maj Eskridge was the pilot assigned to this Nighthawk, although it was routinely flown by others throughout the campaign. 85-0830 presently serves with the 49th FW's 8th FS.

15

F-117A 85-0832 *ONCE BITTEN*, assigned to Capt Andy Nichols, 416th TFS/37th TFW(P), King Khalid RSAFB, February 1991

Capt 'Drew' Nichols flew this aircraft from Tonopah to Saudi Arabia in December 1990 when his squadron was deployed to bolster the ranks of the 37th TFW(P). In six weeks of combat during *Desert Storm*, 85-0832 logged 30 missions. This aircraft saw combat with the 49th FW's 8th FS during Operation *Allied Force* in 1999, and it is still assigned to the unit today.

16

F-117A 85-0834 *NECROMANCER*, assigned to Maj Jeffrey Moore, 416th TFS/37th TFW(P), King Khalid RSAFB, February 1991

The unusually named *NECROMANCER* logged 34 combat missions over Iraq and Kuwait in *Desert Storm*. During the course of one of these missions, Capt Moore came under fire from Syrian gun emplacements while flying close to the border en route to a target in Iraq. Also a *Just Cause* veteran, this jet is also presently assigned to the 49th FW's 8th FS.

17
F-117A 86-0837 *HABU II*, assigned to Capt Matthew Byrd, 416th TFS/37th TFW(P), King Khalid RSAFB, February 1991

HABU II, which displayed 31 mission symbols by war's end, was named by its crew chief, Sgt Dick Pfeifer. He had previously worked on SR-71s at Kadena air base, on Okinawa, where the Lockheed reconnaissance jet was known as the Habu after a venomous snake found locally on the island. Soon after *Desert Storm*, Capt Byrd became a member of the USAF's elite Thunderbirds formation display team, flying in the No 3 slot in an F-16 which he called *HABU III*. 86-0837 presently serves with the 49th FW's 7th Training Squadron, although this unit is scheduled to disband in the near future in preparation for the F-117's service retirement in 2008-09.

18
F-117A 86-0838 *MAGIC HAMMER* assigned to Lt Col Greg Gonyea, 416th TFS/37th TFW(P), King Khalid RSAFB, February 1991

CO of the 416th FS, Lt Col Gonyea used this aircraft to attack Scud missile sites during *Desert Storm*. Gonyea was also instrumental in perfecting the simultaneous multi-aircraft attacks on targets that required more than two bombs to take them out. 86-0838, which flew 36 missions over enemy territory during *Desert Storm*, presently serves with the 49th FW's 8th FS.

19
F-117A 86-0839 *MIDNIGHT REAPER*, assigned to Maj Joseph Salata, 415th TFS/37th TFW(P), King Khalid RSAFB, February 1991

Featuring unusually small 'TR' ruddervator codes and a larger than standard TAC emblem, this aircraft flew a total of 32 combat missions. Maj Salata was still serving with the wing when it was redesignated the 49th FW at Holloman AFB, New Mexico, in July 1992. He later commanded the wing's 9th FS, based at the same location. 86-0839 is currently on strength with the 49th FW's 9th FS in New Mexico.

20
F-117A 88-0841 *Mystic Warrior*, assigned to Maj Rod Shrader, 416th TFS/37th TFW(P), King Khalid RSAFB, January 1991

According to Shrader, this aircraft was unpopular with pilots at King Khalid because of its highly sensitive tracker (finger button). He, nevertheless, flew 18 combat missions with it over Iraq and Kuwait. On one of his more memorable sorties, Maj Shrader used 88-0841 to drop a GBU-27 on the IrAF's HQ building, scoring a direct hit. The laser-guided bomb crashed through eight floors before exploding, blowing out all four sides of the building. 88-0841 is currently on strength with the 49th FW's 9th FS.

21
F-117A 88-0842 *IT'S HAMMERTIME*, assigned to Capt Richard Cline, 416th TFS/37th TFW(P), King Khalid RSAFB, February 1991

The penultimate F-117 built, this aircraft arrived in Saudi Arabia with the 416th TFS in early December 1990. Displaying 33 mission symbols, 88-0842 subsequently saw action with the 49th FW's 8th FS in *Allied Force*. It was still serving with this unit when it went back into action over Iraq from Al Udeid during Operation *Iraqi Freedom* in 2003. Completing a further 16 combat missions in OIF, the Nighthawk is still presently serving with the 8th FS.

BIBLIOGRAPHY

BOOKS
Correll, John T, *The Air Force in the Vietnam War*, Air Force Association, 2004
Coyne, James P, *Airpower in the Gulf*, Air Force Association, 1992
Miller, Jay, *Skunk Works*, Aerofax/Midland, 1995
Morse, Stan, *Gulf Air War Debrief*, Aerospace, 1991
Myers, M/Sgt Harold P and Col Alton Whitley, *Nighthawks over Iraq, Chronology of F-117A Operations in Desert Shield and Desert Storm*, USAF, 1992
Thompson, Warren E, *Bandits Over Baghdad*, Specialty Press, 2000

MAGAZINES AND PERIODICALS
Airman Magazine, July 1990
Lockheed Horizons, 'We Own the Night', Issue No 30, May 1992
World Air Power Journal, Volume 19, Winter 1994

INDEX

References to illustrations are shown in **bold**. Plates are shown with page and caption locators in (brackets).